MASTERING DIFFICULT IV ACCESS:
A Practical Manual

FIRST EDITION

Authors

Admir Hadzic, MD, PhD
Catherine Vandepitte, MD, PhD

Co-Authors

Stien Beyens, MSc
Jirka Cops, PhD
Jill Vanhaeren, MSc
Darren Jacobs, MSc

Contributors

William Aerts, MD | Jonas Bruggen, MD | Robbert Buck, MD
Isabelle Lenders, MD | Ana Lopez Gutiérrez, MD, PhD | Leander Mancel, MD
Simon Njuguna, MD | Fréderic Polus, MD | Sarah Shiba, MD
Walter Staelens, MD | Sam Van Boxstael, MD | Imré Van Herreweghe, MD

Publishing Division of NYSORA, Inc
2585 Broadway, suite 183, New York, NY10025
info@nysora.com, www.nysora.com

Copyright 2024 by Nysora, Inc. All rights reserved. No part of this publication can be reproduced or distributed in any form or by any means, or stored in a database or retrieval system, without the prior written permission of the publisher.

Notice / Disclaimer

The practice of medicine is continuously changing. As new information becomes available, changes in clinical practice and IV access techniques are required. The authors and the publisher of this work have checked with sources believed to be reliable in their efforts to provide information that is in line with the available standards at the time of publication. However, in view of the possibility of human error or changes in medical practice, neither the authors, the publisher, nor any other party who have been involved in the preparation or publication of this work warrants that the information contained herein is accurate or complete. Likewise, they disclaim all responsibility for any errors or omissions, or results obtained from the use of the information contained in this work. Users of the work are encouraged to corroborate the information contained herein with other sources. Readers are also advised to check the current product information for the equipment used for IV access to be certain that the information contained in this work is accurate. Furthermore, medical practitioners must adhere to the protocols and guidelines established in their respective practices or hospitals, as these may vary and take precedence over general recommendations. The authors advise the readers to fact-check the accuracy of the information and use their own.

Library of Congress Identification

Authors:
Prof. Admir Hadzic, MD, PhD
Catherine Vandepitte, MD, PhD

Editors:
Stien Beyens, MSc
Jirka Cops, PhD
Jill Vanhaeren, MSc
Darren Jacobs, MSc

Title: Mastering Difficult IV Access: A Practical Manual
Description: First Edition, 2024.

Identifiers:
Library of Congress Control Number: 2024931346
ISBN 979-8-9870505-9-0

Dedication

This book is dedicated to students and practitioners of medicine.

Foreword

Mastering the art and technique of intravenous (IV) access stands as a fundamental skill for medical professionals. From nurses to doctors, from emergency department personnel to military medics, the ability to efficiently and effectively establish IV access is a cornerstone of patient care. IV access is pivotal in numerous medical settings - for administering medications, fluid therapy, or diagnostics. Efficient and effective IV placement is crucial; it saves valuable time, reduces complications, and fosters professional trust and patient safety.

Yet, despite its critical importance, we have observed a notable gap in practical education and resources dedicated to this vital technical skill, particularly for those encountering difficult IV access scenarios.

As anesthesiologists, we have witnessed firsthand the struggles that younger medical professionals face when attempting IV access. This observation sparked a realization: the need for a comprehensive, practical guide dedicated to the art and science of IV access. Our search for existing resources left us underwhelmed and motivated us to create what we felt was missing - a definitive manual focused on the practical aspects of IV access.

This book is born out of a desire to fill this educational void. It is not just another theoretical textbook; it is a practical manual, rich in visuals and real-world examples, specifically tailored to address the challenges of difficult IV access. We have compiled the most instructional cases from our extensive clinical experience, focusing particularly on those that present unique challenges and require innovative strategies.

Within these pages, you will find a wealth of information, from the basics of anatomy relevant to IV access to patient-specific techniques and best practices. This manual is designed to be a practical resource, aiding both seasoned practitioners and those new to the field. Whether you are looking to refine your skills or build a strong foundation in IV access, this manual aims to be an indispensable tool in enhancing the quality of care you provide.

We are proud to present this manual as a contribution to the medical community. It is a reflection of NYSORA's commitment to improving patient care through education and practical knowledge sharing. We invite our readers to engage with us and to send suggestions for improvements, corrections, or additions to info@nysora.com. Your feedback is invaluable in our ongoing effort to enhance this resource and, in turn, teach the art and skill of IV access.

On behalf of our educational team, Drs Admir Hadzic and Catherine Vandepitte.

Acknowledgments

As we present "Mastering Difficult IV Access: A Practical Manual," our hearts are filled with gratitude toward the many individuals and teams whose dedication, expertise, and passion have brought this project to fruition.

First and foremost, we extend our deepest appreciation to the entire NYSORA Press, New York, NY publishing division. Your unwavering support and commitment to excellence have been the backbone of this endeavor.

A heartfelt congratulations and a huge thank you to our incredible scientific and educational team: Stien Beyens, Dr. Jirka Cops, Jill Vanhaeren, and Darren Jacobs. You have carried the weight of this project on your shoulders, and your contributions have been nothing short of extraordinary and deserve the co-authorship title.

A special acknowledgment goes to our art division, led by the talented Ismar Ruznic and Haris Gusinac. Your artistic vision has brought the pages of this manual to life in ways that words alone could not.

Our design team, under the leadership of Nenad Markovic and comprising the creative talents of Ana Tomic, Aleksa Kostic, and Amar Suljevic, deserves a round of applause. Your eye for detail and design expertise have been instrumental in creating a manual that is not only informative but also visually engaging.

We are immensely thankful to our video production team, including Michel Broekmeulen, Ernad Lokvancic, and Anastasis Petrellis. Your ability to capture and present complex procedures in an accessible format has been crucial in enhancing the learning experience for our readers.

Our gratitude extends to Sabina Saljic, the business lead of VisionExpo.Design. Your strategic insights and leadership have been invaluable in bringing this project to a wider audience.

To our marketing team, Ela Cekic and Aida Vladusic, thank you for your tireless efforts in promoting our manual and ensuring its reach to all corners of the medical community.

To the nurses of the NYSORA Europe team (Deborah Brouwers, Kristel Broux, Ilse Cardinaels, Joëlle Caretta, Hüda Erdem, Marc Houben, Sydney Herfs, Elke Janssen, Ellen Lodewijks, Birgit Lohmar, Natalia Osypova, Mohamed Rafiq, Valerie Vanderlinden, and Ine Vanweert), and each and every one of you who played a part in making "Mastering Difficult IV Access: A Practical Manual" a reality, we are eternally grateful. Your collective efforts have culminated in a manual that will undoubtedly enhance the skills and knowledge of medical professionals worldwide and help benefit many patients.

Authors:

Prof. Admir Hadzic, MD, PhD
Catherine Vandepitte, MD, PhD

Table of Contents

Introduction 10

1. KEY INSIGHTS INTO INTRAVENOUS CANNULATION 11
    1.1 Intravenous catheterization 12
    1.2 Indications for IV catheterization 12
    1.3 Contraindications: When to avoid IV catheterization 12
    1.4 Decision-making process to select the correct catheter and IV therapy 13

2. ANATOMY OF A PERIPHERAL VENOUS CATHETER 14
    2.1 "Over-the-needle" IV catheter design 15
    2.2 IV catheter designs: With or without wings 17
    2.3 Types of peripheral IV catheters 18
        Commonly used peripheral catheter 18
        Midline peripheral catheter 19
    2.4 Finding the perfect fit: Choose the right catheter gauge 20
        How to choose the catheter gauge 23
    2.5 Inspection of the IV 25

3. ANATOMY OF THE VEIN AND THE VENOUS SYSTEM 26
    3.1 Understanding the vein anatomy 27
        Structure 27
        Valves 27
        Types of veins 28
        Vein size 28
        Vein elasticity and fragility 29
        Patient-specific considerations 29
    3.2 Optimal insertion sites for peripheral catheter placement 30
        Upper extremity 32
            Brachial vein 32
            Median cubital vein 33
            Median antebrachial vein 33
            Cephalic vein 33
            Basilic vein 34
            Dorsal metacarpal veins 34
            Commonly used sites for IV cannulation in the upper extremity 35
        Lower extremity 36
            Femoral vein (for large catheters) 37
            Great saphenous vein 37
            Lesser (small) saphenous vein 37
            Dorsal venous arch of the foot 38
            Commonly used sites for IV cannulation in the lower extremity 38

4. MASTERING THE TECHNIQUE OF PERIPHERAL IV CATHETERIZATION 41

4.1 Getting ready: Steps to take before the IV cannulation 42
- Patient identification and preparation 42
- Have the equipment ready 42
  - Optional equipment 43
  - Additional considerations 43
- Catheter-securement devices 43
- IV starter kits 44
- Select the best cannula size 44
- Hand hygiene and gloves 45

4.2 The art and technique of IV catheter insertion 45
- The technique and fine art of tourniquet tightening 46
  - What is a tourniquet? 46
  - Apply the tourniquet 46
- Choose the perfect spot: guide to vein selection 49
- Proper insertion site disinfection 51
- Hold it steady: ensuring vein stability 52
- Use a low angle 52
- Nailing the needle insertion 53
  - What should it feel like? 54
- Alternative approaches to vein cannulation 54
  - Paravenous approach 54
  - Insertion through a bifurcation 55
- Look out for the blood flashback and advance the catheter 55

4.3 Post-insertion procedure and catheter care 56
- Retract the needle and attach the iv tubing 56
- Release the tourniquet and secure the catheter 57

4.4 Algorithm 58

5. COMMON MISTAKES AND TROUBLESHOOTING 61

5.1 Steering clear of common mistakes 62
- Wrong choice of the catheter (A too-short catheter) 62
- Inadequate depth of the needle-catheter system in the vein 62
- Too steep angle of needle insertion 63
- Hematoma formation after catheter removal following an unsuccessful attempt 63
- Starting too proximally on the vein 64
- Failure to secure catheter after insertion 65

5.2 Cannulating complex veins 65
- Difficult or invisible superficial veins 65

   Deep veins 68
   Tortuous or twisted veins.. 69
   Blown veins 70
 5.3 Troubleshooting failed cannulation... 71
 5.4 Avoid vein cannulation at valves... 72
 5.5 What to do when the catheter cannot be advanced... 73
 5.6 IV fluid does not flow 74
 5.7 Large vein cannulation with a large-bore IV catheter 75
 5.8 Algorithms.. 78

6. IV CATHETERIZATION IN LESS COMMON ANATOMICAL SITES 81
 6.1 Cannulation of veins in the foot.. 82
   Saphenous vein cannulation 84
 6.2 Superficial veins over the chest, breast, and thigh area 86
 6.3 Intraosseous cannulation 89

7. IV ACCESS IN SPECIAL POPULATIONS 90
 7.1 IV access in pediatric patients... 91
   Scalp vein cannulation 93
 7.2 IV access in elderly patients 94
 7.3 IV access in underweight patients..100
 7.4 IV access in obese patients..100
 7.5 IV access in patients with burns 103
 7.6 IV access in patients with diabetes 104
 7.7 IV access in patients with a history of IV drug use 107
 7.8 IV access in patients with a history of cancer or chemotherapy treatment 108
 7.9 IV access in emergency settings...109

8. COMPLICATIONS OF IV CANNULATION 111
 8.1 Phlebitis and thrombophlebitis..112
 8.2 Infiltration..113
 8.3 Extravasation 115
 8.4 Hematoma 116
 8.5 IV-associated infection 118
 8.6 Intra-arterial injection 119
 8.7 Air embolism 120

9. ULTRASOUND-GUIDED PERIPHERAL VENOUS ACCESS 122
 9.1 Indications for ultrasound-guided peripheral IV cannulation 123
 9.2 Transducer-needle orientation..124
   In-Plane..124
   Out-of-Plane..124
 9.3 Technique...125
   Patient preparation..125

- Ultrasound setup 126
- Scan the vein 126
- Pre-insertion considerations 127
- Needle insertion...127
- Catheter advancement 129
- Securement 130
- 9.4 Tips 130
- 9.5 Algorithm 131

10. IV CATHETERIZATION IN THE CENTRAL VENOUS SYSTEM 132
- 10.1 Types of central venous catheters...133
  - Peripherally inserted central catheter (PICC) 133
  - Central venous catheter (CVC) 134
    - Tunneled catheter 134
    - Non-tunneled catheter 135
    - Implantable port 136
  - Umbilical catheter..136
- 10.2 External or internal jugular vein...137
  - External jugular vein (EJV) 137
    - Here are the key steps for successful EJV cannulation 138
  - Internal jugular vein (IJV) 140
    - Here are the key steps for successful IJV cannulation 140
- 10.3 Subclavian vein 143
  - Technique using external landmarks...143
  - Ultrasound-Guided Technique 144
- 10.4 Femoral vein cannulation 147
  - Here are the key steps for successful femoral vein cannulation 147

11. IV ACCESS TRAINING AND ASSISTANCE TOOLS 149
- 11.1 IV access simulators 150
- 11.2 Vein finders...151
  - How do they work? 151
  - When to use? 152
  - Practical tips for using vein finders..152
  - Benefits...152
  - Limitations and considerations 152

12. ADDITIONAL SUGGESTED READING 153

Introduction

A few years ago, we at NYSORA produced a video tutorial on intravenous (IV) cannulation techniques and shared it on our YouTube channel. The response was staggering—it garnered over 2 million views! This incredible engagement highlighted a significant gap: the need for a comprehensive, authoritative guide on IV cannulation.

Given the ubiquitous importance of IV therapy, you might think there would be an abundance of instructional resources. But to our surprise, our thorough research revealed a startling dearth of quality materials. Existing resources often lacked the depth, clarity, and practicality we strive for at **NYSORA**. The need for a definitive, high-quality manual on IV access and blood drawing was clear.

And that's precisely what we've created. The book you're holding represents the culmination of our collective expertise and dedication. Welcome to **NYSORA's Mastering Difficult IV Access: A Practical Manual** - a resource we hope will set a new standard in IV access education.

The 6 compelling reasons you need this manual:

The imperative of mastering IV cannulation: A MUST HAVE SKILL for every medical professional

IV cannulation is a seemingly simple yet profoundly important skill. Whether you are a seasoned physician or a budding medical student, understanding and being adept at IV cannulation is not just a skill - it is a fundamental aspect of patient care. If you are considering whether this manual on IV access is for you, let's spell out why this skill is essential for every medical professional, irrespective of rank or specialty.

1. **IV cannulation is done daily:** Regardless of the medical specialty or setting - be it an emergency room (ER), an operating theater, a general ward, or an intensive care unit (ICU) - IV access is everywhere. Medications, fluids, blood products, and vital diagnostics require an IV line.

2. **Patient comfort and safety:** A skilled hand minimizes patient discomfort. More than just the physical pain, repeated unsuccessful attempts can escalate anxiety and distress. Mastering IV cannulation safeguards the patient's veins and emotional well-being.

3. **Efficiency and time-saving:** The ability to secure IV access quickly can mean the difference between life and death. Skilled, efficient cannulation speeds up workflows in non-critical situations, benefiting the medical team and the patient.

4. **Reduction of complications:** IV cannulation, if done improperly, can lead to infections, hematomas, or even more severe complications such as extravasation injuries. Proficiency reduces these risks, ensuring patient safety and reducing potential legal and ethical repercussions.

5. **Professional confidence and trust:** A medical professional skilled at IV cannulation instills confidence in their patients and peers. It is a foundational skill that signals competence in broader medical practices.

6. **Continuous learning and getting better:** The field of medicine is ever-evolving. By committing to learn and refining foundational skills like IV cannulation, you set a precedent for yourself to stay updated, adaptable, and at the forefront of medical practice.

What we teach in this IV Manual

IV access is not just about inserting a needle; it is about understanding the anatomy, recognizing the nuances of each patient's anatomy, and adapting techniques accordingly. This manual explores the topic comprehensively, relying on years of hands-on experience from our clinical team of anesthesiologists and our IV nursing team. While reasonably comprehensive, it aims to be the most PRACTICAL go-to resource for medical professionals at all stages of their careers, ensuring that the art and science of IV cannulation are within everyone's grasp.

In essence, whether you want to refine your skills, understand the underlying principles, or teach others, this manual, written by highly experienced practitioners, can equip you with skills to better your practice and elevate the standard of care you offer to every patient.

01

Scan the QR code for IV technique videos

KEY INSIGHTS INTO INTRAVENOUS CANNULATION

1.1 Intravenous catheterization

Intravenous (IV) catheterization is a crucial medical procedure for patient care, such as in patients requiring rapid treatment administration, consistent medication, or fluid replacement therapy. It plays a vital role in various medical fields and settings, from ERs to surgical centers, and is performed by nearly all healthcare professionals, including nurses, doctors, and paramedics. Proper technique and maintenance of the catheter site are imperative to prevent potential complications, such as hematoma, infection, or thrombophlebitis.

1.2 Indications for IV catheterization

IV access is crucial in healthcare, underpinning numerous therapeutic and diagnostic procedures essential for effective patient care. IV access enables medication infusion for immediate effect, bypassing digestive delays; facilitates fluid replacement for rehydration and electrolyte balance; is vital for prompt blood transfusions in cases of significant blood loss; aids in enhancing imaging studies' precision through contrast dye injections; allows monitoring of vital hemodynamic parameters in severe cases; provides essential nutrients for those unable to eat; proves indispensable in emergencies for delivering crucial treatments; and is used for administering anesthesia.

1.3 Contraindications: When to avoid IV catheterization

Avoiding IV access in limbs with certain conditions is crucial for several reasons, each related to minimizing the risk of complications, ensuring the effectiveness of treatment, and protecting patient safety. Here's a rationale for each specified condition:

- **Skin infections, burns, recent trauma, or surgeries:** These conditions compromise the integrity of the skin and underlying tissues, increasing the infection risk and further trauma. IV insertion in such areas can also be more painful and may interfere with the healing process.
- **Edema:** Edema indicates fluid accumulation that can affect tissue perfusion and may obscure veins, making IV insertion more difficult and increasing the risk of complications.
- **Phlebitis or thrombophlebitis:** Inserting an IV into a vein that is inflamed (phlebitis) or has a clot (thrombophlebitis) can exacerbate the condition, leading to further vein damage, increased pain, and the potential for embolic events.
- **Compromised circulation:** Limbs with compromised circulation are at higher risk for complications because the reduced blood flow can impair healing and increase the infection risk. IV therapy might also be less effective if medications or fluids are not distributed efficiently.
- **History of deep vein thrombosis (DVT):** Inserting an IV in a limb with a history of DVT increases the risk of dislodging a clot, which could lead to serious complications, such as a pulmonary embolism.
- **Prior surgical interventions:** Limbs that have undergone surgery may have altered anatomy or circulation, increasing the risk of complications from IV insertion.
- **Arteriovenous (AV) fistula:** An AV fistula is typically created for dialysis access in patients with renal failure. Using a limb with an AV fistula for IV access can damage the fistula, compromising its longevity and function for dialysis.
- **Paralysis:** Limbs affected by paralysis may have altered sensation, making it difficult to detect complications related to IV therapy, such as infiltration or infection. Additionally, circulation may be compromised in paralyzed limbs.

Avoiding IV placement in these conditions is essential to prevent complications such as infections, impaired healing, thrombosis, and damage to critical vascular access points. It ensures that IV therapy is both safe and effective for the patient.

1.4 Decision-making process to select the correct catheter and IV therapy

In the traditional approach to IV therapy, the selection of the most appropriate venous access is often overlooked. The lack of pre-catheterization planning may necessitate re-cannulation, and if peripheral access becomes untenable, the consideration for transitioning to a central venous catheter arises. With a 'proactive approach,' the most suitable catheter choice is determined by an initial evaluation based on the nature of the therapy and the patient's condition. Factors such as the types of infusion fluids (osmolarity and pH), medications, and potential complications associated with their use are integral to this decision-making process. This decision-making model is predicated on the interplay of three key factors: the appropriate catheter selection, the patient's history and current condition, and the nature and duration of the therapy.

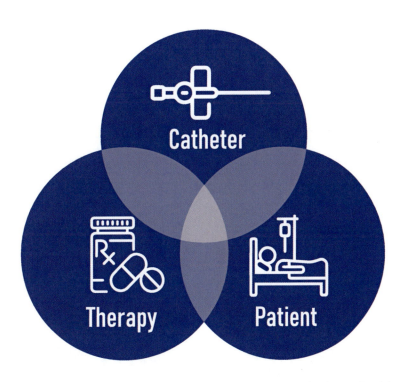

Fig-1-01. This decision-making model to select the correct catheter and IV therapy is predicated on the interplay of three key factors: the appropriate catheter selection, the patient's history and current condition, and the nature and duration of the therapy.

02

Scan the QR code for IV technique videos

ANATOMY OF A PERIPHERAL VENOUS CATHETER

2.1 "Over-the-needle" IV catheter design

There are two major groups of IV devices: the "over-the-needle" catheter and the "butterfly needle". This manual will focus on the "over-the-needle" catheter, which is by far the most common, focusing on starting an IV infusion. This type of IV catheter is designed for short-term use, typically lasting up to a couple of days (typically four days).

Fig-2-02. An "over-the-needle" catheter. Note the catheter that is sleeved over the steel needle (stylet).

Main components of an IV catheter
- A flexible plastic tube called a **catheter or cannula** is suitable for insertion into the lumen of a vein, where it stays indwelling for the intended therapy.
- A hollow metal needle, called the **stylet**, punctures the skin and the vein to allow sliding of the catheter into the vein.
- The catheter is made from a flexible and biocompatible material such as Teflon or polyurethane, reducing the risk of phlebitis.

Catheter design overview
- The catheter tightly fits over the stylet to facilitate sliding the catheter over the needle when inserted into a vein.
- The needle's metal tip extends slightly beyond the catheter's tip, usually by about 1-2 mm.
- This design facilitates needle entry through the skin and into the vein first, followed by the catheter entry and sliding into the vein.
- The needle and the catheter must both be in the lumen of the vein before the catheter can be slid over the needle deeper into the vein.
- Once the catheter is sufficiently slid into the lumen, the needle is withdrawn, leaving the catheter in place.
- The catheter serves as the channel for fluid or medication administration.

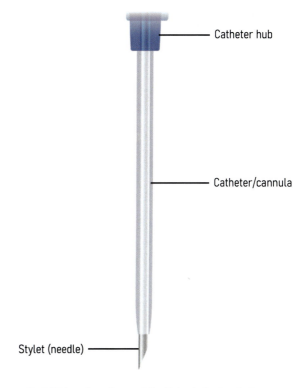

Fig-2-03. In an "over-the-needle" catheter design the plastic cannula slides over the stylet.

02 Anatomy of a peripheral venous catheter

Fig-2-04. IV catheters are available in different gauge sizes and lengths. The size of the catheter and length are chosen based on the peripheral IV flow rate, the technique of insertion, and the depth of the veins.

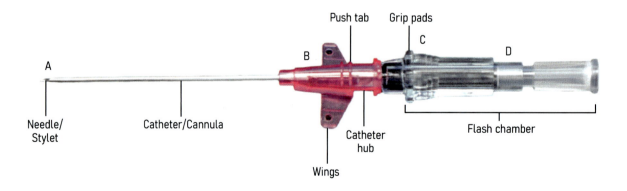

Fig-2-05. Components of the IV needle-catheter system. A) This part must be inserted into the vein before the catheter can be slid. B) Wings are used to secure the catheter to the skin by taping or suturing. C) The catheter is held by grip pads during insertion. D) Appearance of blood in the flashback chamber indicates proper insertion in the lumen of the vein.

- **Catheter hub:** The proximal end that remains outside the body. It provides a connection point for a syringe or IV tubing for medication delivery or IV infusion.
- **Flash chamber:** As the needle enters the vein, the chamber fills with blood as a visual indicator of correct needle and catheter placement. A flash chamber may also include a safety valve that prevents unintended blood spills, and allows air to vent to prevent "air trapping", which impedes the IV flow.
- **Grip pads:** The grip pad allows for a secure grip during the IV needle-catheter system insertion, aiding accuracy and confidence during the procedure.
- **Push tab:** A user-friendly component designed for effortless catheter advancement using a (usually index) finger.
- **Wings:** The wings on the catheter provide a stable and secure surface for attaching medical tape, keeping the catheter firmly in place. **Note:** Not all catheters have a wings design.

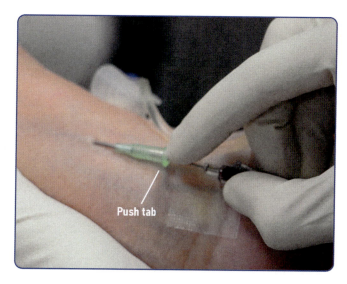

Fig-2-06. The tab on the IV catheter is used to "push" or advance the catheter into the vein over the needle, usually using the index finger.

2.2 IV catheter designs: With or without wings

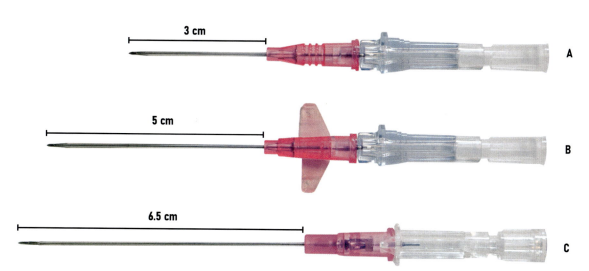

Fig-2-07. IV catheters with (B) or without (A, C) wings and with varying lengths.

IV catheters are designed to deliver medications or withdraw blood directly into or from the bloodstream, respectively. They come in different designs, with or without wings, and varying lengths to cater to specific clinical needs and preferences. Generally, catheters with wings are used for prolonged catheter use (days), whereas those without wings are for short-term use (hours), i.e. for rehydration.

With or without wings: Catheters may come with "wings" or flanges, which provide a better grip for the healthcare provider during insertion and securement of the catheter. Wings also facilitate the stabilization of the catheter on the patient's skin, reducing the risk of accidental dislodgement. Catheters without wings are typically used in settings where space is limited or when the catheter is intended for very short-term use.

Varying lengths: The length of IV catheters can vary significantly, from short peripheral catheters intended for superficial veins to long central venous catheters designed for insertion into larger, central veins. The choice of length depends on the intended duration of use, the type of therapy or medication being administered, and the patient's anatomy. Longer catheters are generally used for treatments requiring central venous access or for patients with difficult peripheral venous access.

Ease of handling and stabilization

- Wings or flaps are often present in peripheral IV catheters. These wings or flaps make the catheter easier to insert, especially when using the one-handed technique.
- They also provide a flat surface that can be taped or sutured to the skin, providing additional security for the catheter once it is in place.
- Catheters without wings are often used when additional surface area is not required for stabilization or when a catheter needs to be inserted quickly.
- Catheters are often secured with an adhesive dressing, or taped to the skin.
- Peripheral IV catheters, inserted into smaller veins in the hands, arms, feet, or scalp, often have wings. These sites are more mobile and benefit from the additional stabilization the wings provide.

Duration of use

Catheters intended for short-term use might be simpler in design without wings, while those intended for more prolonged use have wings for better stabilization.

Preference and tradition

The choice of the catheter is often on the indications and clinicians' and institution's preferences.

2.3 Types of peripheral IV catheters

Intravenous catheters are indispensable tools in healthcare, designed to administer medications, fluids, and nutrients directly into the bloodstream, as well as for blood withdrawal. Their variety in shapes, sizes, and designs allows them to meet a wide array of clinical needs, ensuring that patients receive the most appropriate and effective IV therapy based on their specific conditions.

Peripheral IV catheters These are the most frequently used IV catheters and are designed for short-term use. They are inserted into peripheral veins, such as those in the hands or arms, and are ideal for immediate access to the bloodstream for the infusion of medications, fluids, or blood sampling. The selection of the right peripheral IV catheter depends on the patient's vein size and the viscosity and volume of the fluid or medication to be administered. They come in various gauges (diameters) and lengths to accommodate different patient needs, with smaller gauges (larger diameters) used for thicker, more viscous fluids or rapid fluid replacement.

The best catheter for each indication is chosen based on the patient's vein size and the type of fluid or medication to be administered.

Commonly used peripheral catheter

- **Location:** Inserted into peripheral veins (usually in the arm or hand).
- **Use:** Short-term (up to four days) fluid therapy or medication administration.
- **Characteristics:** Short (< 7.6 cm or 3 inches) and small-diameter catheters.

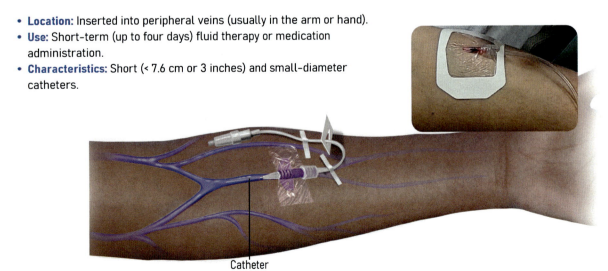

Fig-2-08. Commonly used peripheral catheter.

Midline peripheral catheter

Longer than a short, commonly used peripheral IV catheter but shorter than a central venous catheter.
- **Location:** Inserted in the antecubital area or in the upper arm and positioned with the tip near the axilla.
- **Use:** Medium-term use for IV therapies lasting from one week to one month. Do not use these for strong medications such as chemotherapy, as these could damage the peripheral nervous system.
- **Characteristics:** Midlines are usually about 8-12 cm (3-5 inches) long. Unlike central lines, their tips do not extend into the central veins near the chest. A midline catheter is usually inserted into a large-lumen vein (basilic or brachial vein) using ultrasound guidance to reduce the risk of thrombosis, which often occurs with smaller veins.

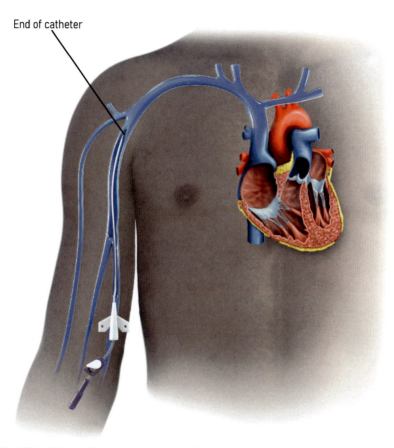

Fig-2-09. A midline peripheral catheter is inserted in the upper arm and positioned with the tip near the axilla.

2.4 Finding the perfect fit: Choose the right catheter gauge

Fig-2-10. Peripheral IV catheters are available in various sizes, typically ranging from 14 to 24 gauge (G), to accommodate different clinical needs and patient populations.

Choosing the correct IV catheter is a foundational step in ensuring a successful cannulation procedure. The selection of the appropriate gauge of a peripheral IV catheter is crucial for optimizing the administration of fluids, medications, blood products, and for conducting certain diagnostic tests. Peripheral IV catheters are available in various sizes, typically ranging from 14 to 26 gauge (G), to accommodate different clinical needs and patient populations.

Understanding gauge sizes
- **14G:** The 14G catheter, being the largest, allows for the highest flow rates. It is typically used in emergency situations where rapid fluid resuscitation is required, such as in cases of severe blood loss. Due to its large size, it may be more painful to insert and is usually reserved for adult patients.
- **16G and 18G:** These sizes are also used for rapid administration of fluids and are common choices for surgery, especially major operations where blood loss is anticipated. They strike a balance between the need for high flow rates and patient comfort.
- **20G and 22G:** These are the most commonly used sizes for a wide range of patients, including adults and children. They are suitable for most IV therapies, including the administration of medications, blood products, and for routine blood draws.
- **24G and 26G:** The smallest gauges, such as 24G and 26G, are typically used for infants, children, or adults with small or fragile veins. While they offer the slowest flow rates, they are less painful to insert and are better suited for patients requiring minimal fluid administration or those with difficult venous access.

The inverse relationship between gauge and diameter

The gauge system might seem counterintuitive at first glance because it describes an inverse relationship: as the gauge number increases, the diameter of the catheter decreases. Therefore, a higher gauge number indicates a thinner catheter.

Clinical considerations

When selecting the gauge of a peripheral IV catheter, healthcare professionals consider several factors:

- **Desired flow rate:** Larger diameters (smaller gauge numbers) allow for higher flow rates, which is essential in emergency resuscitation or when administering viscous fluids.
- **Viscosity of the infused substance:** Thicker substances, like some blood products or parenteral nutrition, may require a larger diameter for efficient administration.
- **Patient comfort and vein size:** Smaller gauges are less painful and are better suited for patients with smaller or fragile veins, improving the patient experience and reducing the risk of vein damage.
- **Duration and type of therapy:** The anticipated duration of IV therapy and the type of medication can also influence the choice of catheter size. Some medications can irritate the vein's lining and may require a slower infusion rate or a larger vein to dilute the medication more effectively.

In summary, selecting the appropriate gauge for a peripheral IV catheter is a critical decision that impacts the success of the cannulation procedure, the effectiveness of the therapy, and the comfort and safety of the patient. Understanding the relationship between gauge size and catheter diameter, along with the clinical needs of the patient, allows healthcare professionals to make informed choices in venous access.

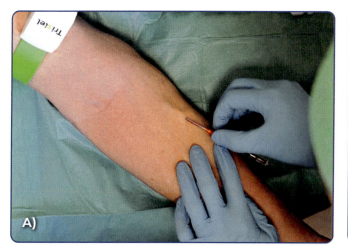
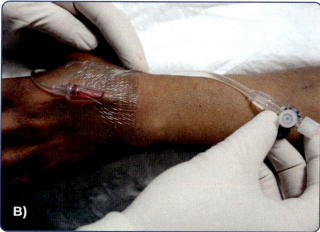

Fig-2-11. A) The 14G (orange) catheter, being the largest, allows for the highest flow rates. B) The 20G IV (pink) catheter is one of the most commonly used sizes for a wide range of patients, including adults and children. They are suitable for most IV therapies, including the administration of medications, blood products, and for routine blood draws.

02 Anatomy of a peripheral venous catheter

GAUGE (G)	DIAMETER (mm)	MAXIMUM FLOW RATE (mL/min)	RECOMMENDED USE	NOTES
14G ORANGE	2.00	270	Adult patients: • Trauma • Surgery • Rapid blood transfusion	Suitable for large volume resuscitation
16G GREY	1.80	236	Adult patients: • Trauma • Surgery • Rapid fluid resuscitation • Rapid blood transfusion	Suitable for large volume resuscitation
18G GREEN	1.30	75-120	Adult patients: • Surgery • Rapid fluid resuscitation • Rapid blood transfusion	Suitable for most standard IV therapies
20G PINK	1.10	40-80	Adult patients: • Blood transfusion • Long-term IV therapy • Routine medication administration	Suitable for most standard IV therapies
22G BLUE	0.90	56	Pediatric patients or adults/elderly with small or fragile veins	Suitable for basic IV therapy
24G YELLOW	0.60	36	Neonates and infants: • Blood transfusions • Basic IV therapy	Will not accommodate rapid flow rates
26G PURPLE	0.46	13-15	Neonates and premature infants	

Table 1. Overview of common gauge sizes and colors.

How to choose the catheter gauge

The gauge of the catheter determines the maximum flow rate for IV therapy. Even when the infusion is set to "wide open" for maximum flow, the actual flow rate will still be constrained by the catheter's gauge. Please refer to Table 1 and the discussion above for maximum flow rates with different catheter gauges.

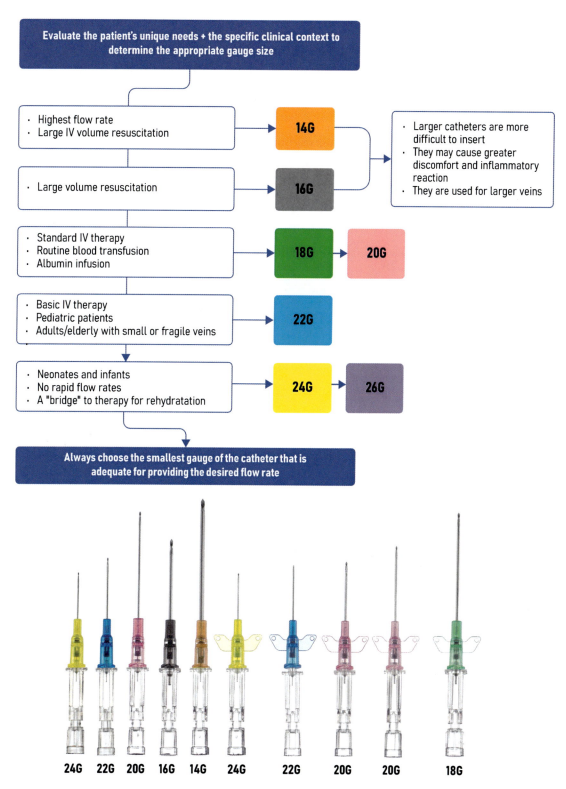

Fig-2-12. Decision-making infographic to guide which needle gauge should be used.

Choosing the right gauge size for an IV catheter is a critical decision in clinical practice, impacting both the efficacy of the therapy delivered and the comfort and safety of the patient.

Here's why opting for the smaller gauge, when appropriate, is considered best practice.

1. Minimizes vein trauma

A smaller gauge needle, being thinner, is less likely to cause significant blowing to the vein into which it is inserted. Larger gauges, while necessary for certain treatments, have a higher risk of causing vein trauma, and complications such as phlebitis or thrombosis. By minimizing vein trauma, the risk of these complications is reduced.

2. Enhances patient comfort

Needle insertion is an invasive procedure that can cause discomfort or pain for the patient. A smaller gauge needle, due to its thinner diameter, typically causes less pain during insertion and while in place. This consideration is especially important in settings where patients may require long-term IV access or have a history of difficult IV access.

3. Improves the patient experience

Reducing the physical discomfort of IV therapy contributes to a better overall patient experience. Patients who have less painful interactions with healthcare systems are more likely to adhere to necessary treatments and have a positive view of their care, which can influence their recovery and health outcomes.

4. Facilitates certain therapies

Some medications and fluids can be safely administered through smaller gauge catheters without compromising the therapy's effectiveness. Using the smallest gauge possible for these therapies ensures patient comfort without affecting the treatment.

However, gauge selection must be individualized:

- **Assessing patient needs:** Not all therapies can be administered through small gauge catheters. The viscosity of the fluid, the required flow rate, and the duration of therapy must be considered. For example, blood transfusions, rapid fluid resuscitation, and the administration of certain high-viscosity drugs may necessitate larger gauge catheters.
- **Clinical context:** The patient's vein size, vein condition, and overall health status (e.g., hydration level, presence of chronic illnesses) influence the appropriate gauge size. In some cases, a larger gauge may be necessary to secure IV access in difficult situations or to ensure that the chosen vein can accommodate the catheter without collapsing.
- **Monitoring and adjustment:** Post-insertion, it's important to monitor the IV site for signs of complications, regardless of the gauge size chosen. If issues arise, reassessment and adjustment of the catheter size or site may be necessary to ensure the ongoing safety and comfort of the patient.

In summary, while the preference for smaller gauge catheters is guided by the principles of minimizing vein trauma and enhancing patient comfort, clinical judgment and individual patient assessment are paramount in determining the most appropriate gauge size for IV therapy. This tailored approach ensures that the benefits of IV treatments are maximized while minimizing potential risks and discomfort for the patient.

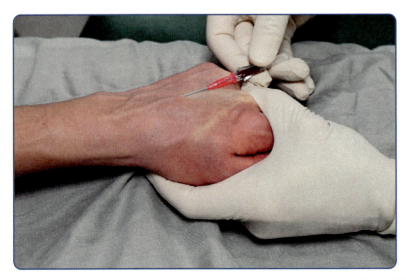

Fig-2-13. Choosing the right gauge size for an IV catheter is a critical decision in clinical practice, impacting both the efficacy of the therapy delivered and the comfort and safety of the patient. A smaller gauge needle (20G), being thinner, is less likely to cause significant damage to the vein into which it is inserted.

2.5 Inspection of the IV

Regular inspection, replacement, or removal of an IV line after a certain period is a critical practice in healthcare to ensure patient safety and prevent complications. This approach is grounded in several important considerations:

- **Infection control:** One of the primary reasons for the regular inspection and timely replacement of IV lines is to prevent infections, including local site infections and more serious systemic infections like sepsis. The longer an IV catheter remains in place, the greater the risk of bacteria colonizing the catheter and entering the bloodstream.
- **Phlebitis prevention:** Phlebitis, an inflammation of the vein, is a common complication of IV therapy. It can result from mechanical irritation, the chemical irritation of the vein lining by the infused medication, or bacterial infection. Regular assessment helps in early detection and management, reducing the patient's discomfort and preventing further vascular damage.
- **Prevention of occlusion:** IV lines can become occluded (blocked) due to a blood clot or precipitate from the infused fluids or medications. Regular checks ensure that the line remains patent (open and functional), allowing for the effective delivery of medications and fluids.
- **Minimizing the risk of thrombosis:** IV catheters are essentially a foreign body within a vein increases the risk of thrombus (blood clot) formation. This risk grows with the duration the IV catheter is in place. By inspecting and replacing IV lines as needed, healthcare providers can reduce the incidence of thrombosis, which can lead to serious complications if a clot dislodges and travels to the lungs (pulmonary embolism).
- **Ensuring effective treatment:** Regular inspection of the IV line also ensures that the medication or fluid therapy is being delivered effectively. Any issues with the IV line, such as infiltration (where the fluid leaks into the surrounding tissue) or extravasation (where vesicant agents leak into the tissue and cause damage), can be promptly addressed to ensure that the treatment is effective and to minimize tissue damage.
- **Patient comfort:** Regular inspection and timely replacement of IV lines can significantly enhance patient comfort. It allows for the early detection and management of issues like irritation, swelling, or pain at the IV site, improving the overall patient experience.
- **Compliance with guidelines:** Healthcare protocols and guidelines often recommend specific time frames for replacing IV lines to mitigate risks and promote best practices in patient care. Adhering to these guidelines is part of maintaining high standards of care and ensuring patient safety.

In summary, the regular inspection, timely replacement, or removal of IV lines are essential practices that help prevent a range of complications, from infections to thrombosis, ensuring the safety and comfort of the patient while maintaining the effectiveness of the IV therapy.

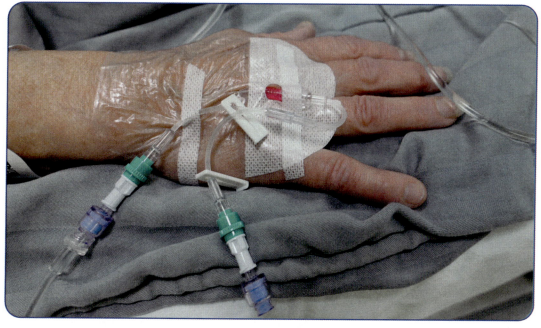

Fig-2-14. Regularly inspect the IV line to prevent infection, phlebitis, and occlusion of the IV line.

03

Scan the QR code for IV technique videos

ANATOMY OF THE VEIN AND THE VENOUS SYSTEM

IV access combines expertise and understanding of the venous anatomy for success and decreases the risk of failure. This chapter reviews the fundamental anatomy of veins and the diverse access sites, each possessing distinct features. The knowledge in this section is important for making informed decisions in clinical settings.

3.1 Understanding the vein anatomy

Understanding vein anatomy is essential for healthcare professionals to achieve successful IV catheter placements. Effective IV therapy not only depends on the skill of the practitioner but also on their knowledge of the vein's structure and how it interacts with the needle and catheter. Here's a deeper look into the components and characteristics of veins that are crucial for IV placement.

Structure

Veins are blood vessels that return deoxygenated blood from the body back to the heart, except for the pulmonary and umbilical veins, which carry oxygenated blood. They are part of the circulatory system, which also includes arteries and capillaries. The structure of veins comprises three main layers:

- **Tunica interna:** The innermost layer, which is smooth to facilitate the easy flow of blood. It includes an endothelial lining that minimizes friction and can be susceptible to damage during IV insertion.
- **Tunica media:** This middle layer is thinner in veins than in arteries. It consists of smooth muscle and elastic fibers, allowing veins to stretch and accommodate varying volumes of blood. Vasoconstriction in stressed, frightened patients makes cannulation more difficult.
- **Tunica externa:** The outer layer made up of connective tissue, which helps anchor the veins to nearby tissues and provides structural support.

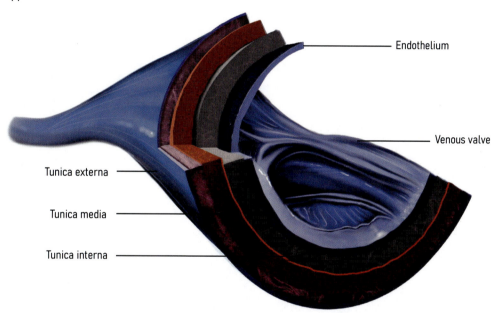

Fig-3-15. Veins exhibit a tri-layered structure: Tunica interna, tunica media (this middle layer is thinner in veins than in arteries and regulates vasoconstriction), and tunica externa. Vasoconstriction in stressed, frightened patients makes cannulation more difficult.

Valves

The valves in peripheral veins play an important role in the circulatory system, primarily facilitating the unidirectional flow of blood back to the heart. Located throughout the veins in limbs and other peripheral areas, these flap-like structures prevent the backflow of blood, ensuring it moves against gravity, especially from the lower extremities. When muscles contract, they squeeze the veins, pushing blood towards the heart. The valves then close to stop the blood from flowing backward, aiding in venous return. This mechanism is vital for maintaining steady blood circulation, preventing venostasis, and reducing the risk of conditions like varicose veins and venous insufficiency.

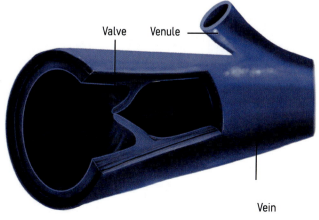

Fig-3-16. A valve in a vein regulates the blood flow.

IV cannulation should be avoided in the vicinity of the valves within peripheral veins for several key reasons. Firstly, the presence of valves can make cannulation more challenging due to the physical obstruction they present, potentially leading to unsuccessful attempts or damage to the vein. Secondly, inserting an IV cannula near a valve can lead to irritation and inflammation of the vein, known as phlebitis, which can compromise the function of the valve and increase the risk of thrombosis. Additionally, the turbulence caused by the cannula near the valve can slow down blood flow, increasing the likelihood of clot formation. Therefore, to minimize complications and ensure effective venous access, it is recommended to choose cannulation sites away from the valves.

Types of veins

Superficial veins
- Located closer to the skin's surface. Less connective tissue makes them more mobile and prone to "rolling".

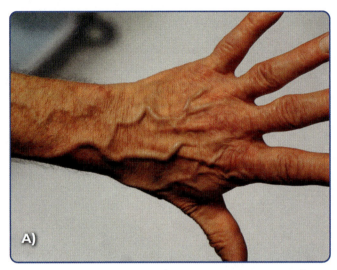
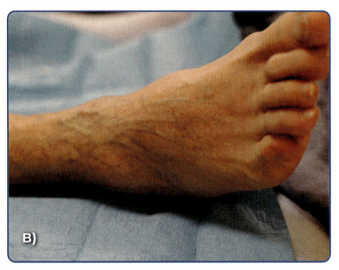

Fig-3-17. A) Superficial veins of the hand and B) superficial foot veins require a small IV gauge to prevent rolling.

Deep veins
- Located deep within the body tissues.
- They typically run alongside arteries.
- Are surrounded by more connective tissue which stabilizes them.

Perforator veins
- Connect the superficial and deep venous systems.
- Primary function: Enable the efficient return of blood from the skin's surface and underlying tissues to the deep veins and heart.
- Equipped with valves that ensure blood flows in one direction from the superficial to the deep veins.
- Essential for maintaining venous pressure gradients and for the prevention of venous disorders such as chronic venous insufficiency and varicose veins.

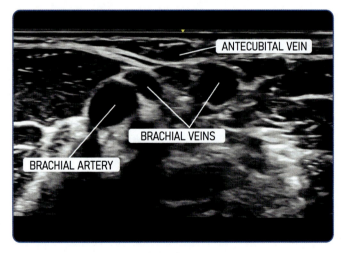

Fig-3-18. The brachial veins lay alongside the brachial artery in the upper arm.

Vein size

Veins play a crucial role in the circulatory system, functioning as conduits to return deoxygenated blood to the heart. Their diameters can vary significantly, from as small as 1 millimeter to as large as 1-1.5 centimeters, depending on their location in the body and their specific role within the venous system. This variability in size is key to their function as capacitance vessels, a term that highlights their ability to stretch and accommodate varying volumes of blood. Below, we discuss the characteristics that define veins, their capacity for vasodilation, and the role of venules, the smallest veins in the body.

Capacitance vessels and vasodilation

Veins are known as capacitance vessels because of their ability to hold more blood than arteries. This is due to the structure of their walls, which are thinner and less muscular than those of arteries but much more flexible. This flexibility allows veins to expand (vasodilation) and increase their capacity to hold blood, which is crucial for maintaining blood volume and pressure within the circulatory system.

The ability of veins to act as blood reservoirs is particularly important. In times of need, such as during physical exertion or in response to hemorrhage, veins can constrict (vasoconstriction) to mobilize stored blood back into circulation, thereby ensuring that vital organs continue to receive an adequate supply of oxygen and nutrients. This reservoir function is facilitated by the venous system's inherent elasticity and compliance, allowing for significant variations in blood volume without large changes in blood pressure.

Venules: The initial collectors

At the microcirculatory level, venules play a pivotal role. These smallest veins in the body serve as the initial collectors of blood from the capillary beds, where exchange of gases, nutrients, and waste products occurs between the blood and tissues. Venules receive oxygen-depleted, nutrient-depleted blood from the capillaries and begin the process of transporting it back toward the heart.

As blood moves through the venules, it gradually enters larger and larger veins, eventually reaching the major veins of the body – the inferior and superior vena cava. These two large veins are responsible for carrying blood from the lower and upper parts of the body, respectively, into the right atrium of the heart. From there, blood is sent to the right ventricle and then to the lungs for oxygenation before being redistributed to the body.

The significance of vein diameter

The diameter of a vein plays a critical role in its function. Smaller veins, including venules, are more numerous and are primarily involved in collecting blood from capillaries. As veins converge and increase in diameter, they become fewer in number but increase in capacity, allowing them to transport larger volumes of blood toward the heart. The variation in diameter also affects the pressure and speed of blood flow, with larger veins facilitating the smooth and efficient return of blood to the heart under lower pressure.

In summary

Understanding the anatomy and function of veins, from the smallest venules to the largest capacitance vessels, is essential for appreciating the complexity and efficiency of the circulatory system. Veins' ability to act as reservoirs and their capacity for vasodilation and vasoconstriction are fundamental to maintaining hemodynamic stability, ensuring that the body can adapt to varying demands and conditions by regulating blood volume and pressure.

Vein elasticity and fragility

Veins are more elastic and less rigid than arteries, making them more difficult to puncture accurately. Their elasticity allows them to accommodate varying blood volumes but also means they can easily collapse if not handled properly. Additionally, veins can be fragile, particularly in elderly patients or those with certain health conditions, increasing the risk of bruising or damage during IV insertion.

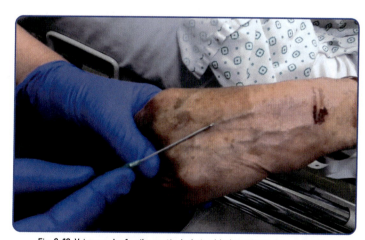

Fig-3-19. Veins can be fragile, particularly in elderly patients, increasing the risk of bruising or damage during IV insertion.

Patient-specific considerations

A thorough understanding of vein anatomy must be complemented by patient-specific considerations. For instance, patients with chronic illnesses, those undergoing chemotherapy, or individuals with a history of IV drug use may have veins that are more difficult to access. When planning an IV cannulation, incorporating patient-specific considerations is essential for a successful outcome and minimizing potential complications. These considerations include:

- **Age and skin integrity:**
  - Elderly patients may have fragile, thin skin and delicate veins, necessitating the use of smaller gauge cannulas and a gentler approach.
  - Pediatric patients require appropriately sized equipment and techniques tailored to manage their fear and anxiety.
- **Chronic conditions:**
  - Patients with conditions like diabetes or vascular diseases might have compromised veins, making careful site selection critical.
- **Hydration status:**
  - Dehydration can render veins difficult to palpate and cannulate, highlighting the importance of assessing the patient's hydration before proceeding.
- **Previous cannulations:**
  - A history of frequent cannulations can lead to scarred or thrombosed veins, requiring thorough examination to identify viable cannulation sites.
- **Medical history:**
  - Knowledge of allergies to cannula materials or dressings is important to prevent adverse reactions.
- **Patient comfort and mobility:**
  - Consider the patient's comfort, mobility, and the anticipated duration of IV therapy to choose the most suitable cannulation site.
- **Vein selection:**
  - Avoid areas of flexion to reduce the risk of cannula displacement and complications.
  - Consider the use of ultrasound guidance for patients with difficult venous access.

Incorporating these considerations into the planning phase of IV cannulation ensures not only the technical success of the procedure but also enhances patient comfort and satisfaction.

In conclusion, a comprehensive understanding of vein anatomy is fundamental to effective IV placement. It allows healthcare professionals to make informed decisions about vein selection, navigate the challenges of IV insertion, and provide high-quality care, minimizing discomfort and complications for the patient.

3.2 Optimal insertion sites for peripheral catheter placement

Choosing the optimal vein for IV cannulation is a nuanced process that requires consideration of various factors, including the patient's anatomy, the clinical reason for IV therapy, and the healthcare provider's expertise and preference. This decision-making process is critical for ensuring the effectiveness of the treatment, minimizing discomfort, and reducing the risk of complications. Below is a practical consideration of how these factors influence the selection of the best vein for IV cannulation.

Patient's body structure

The physical characteristics of the patient play a significant role in vein selection. Factors such as the size and visibility of veins, skin condition, and the presence of any previous venous access sites or scars can affect the choice. For instance, patients with larger, more visible veins may offer more options for cannulation sites. In contrast, those with smaller or less visible veins may present a challenge, requiring a more experienced clinician to perform the cannulation.

Reason for the IV

The purpose of the IV therapy significantly influences the choice of the cannulation site. For example:

- **Emergency situations:** In emergencies, where rapid fluid administration is necessary, larger veins, such as those in the antecubital fossa (the front of the elbow), may be preferred due to their larger diameter and higher flow rate capability.
- **Long-term therapy:** For patients requiring long-term IV therapy, such as chemotherapy, veins in the forearm might be chosen to preserve larger veins for future use and to enhance patient comfort.
- **Pediatric patients:** In pediatric patients, scalp veins or veins in the hands and feet might be considered due to their accessibility and the smaller size of the patient.

Experience and choice

The healthcare provider's skill level and experience with IV cannulation play a crucial role in vein selection. Clinicians with extensive experience are often more adept at assessing the quality of veins by palpation and visual inspection, enabling them to choose sites that might not be apparent to less experienced providers. Additionally, personal preference, based on previous successes or institutional protocols, may guide the choice of cannulation site.

Commonly preferred IV sites for specific medical reasons

Certain IV sites are commonly preferred for specific treatments or patient populations:

- **Hand and wrist veins:** Often used for short-term therapies, these sites are generally less uncomfortable for the patient and interfere less with mobility.
- **Antecubital fossa veins:** Suitable for situations requiring rapid fluid administration. However, these sites might be less comfortable and more prone to movement, potentially leading to dislodgement of the cannula.
- **Forearm veins:** Preferred for longer-term IV therapy due to their stability and lower risk of complications. They offer a good balance between comfort and functionality.
- **External jugular vein:** May be considered in specific emergencies where peripheral venous access is not achievable.

Conclusion

The selection of a vein for IV cannulation is a critical decision that must be tailored to each patient's unique circumstances, considering their anatomy, the purpose of the IV therapy, and the clinician's expertise. Understanding the advantages and limitations of different venous access sites enables healthcare providers to make informed choices, optimizing patient care and minimizing the risk of complications.

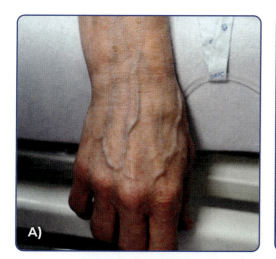
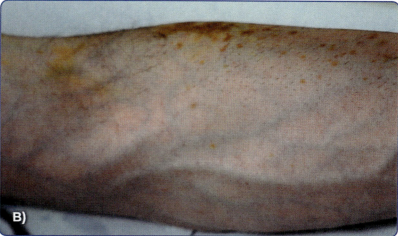
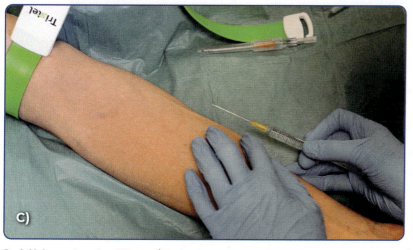
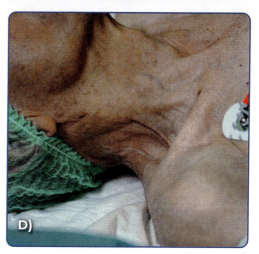

Fig-3-20. Commonly preferred IV sites. A) Hand and wrist veins are often used for short-term therapies. B) Antecubital fossa veins are suitable for situations requiring rapid fluid administration. C) Forearm veins are preferred for longer-term IV therapy. D) The external jugular vein may be considered in specific emergencies where peripheral venous access is not achievable.

Here are some common sites for vein cannulation:

Upper extremity

The upper extremity provides various good venous access sites, each with advantages and considerations. When selecting an appropriate site, practitioners should know the anatomy of these veins and their characteristics. Here's an overview from cranial to caudal.

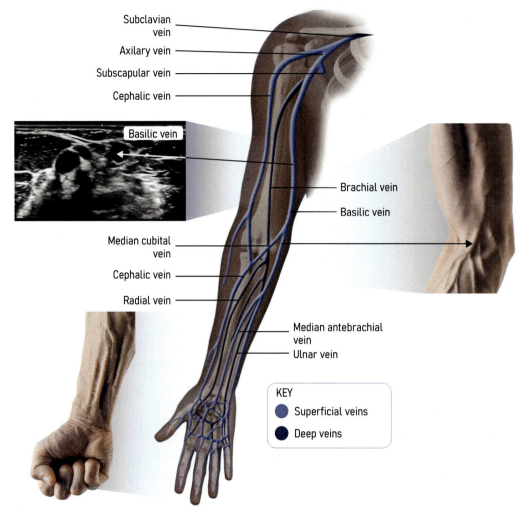

Fig-3-21. Insertion sites for peripheral catheter placement in the upper extremity.

Brachial vein

- **Location:** Typically found in pairs alongside the brachial artery in the upper arm.
- **Advantages:** Provides good blood flow; often used for PICC line placements.
- **Considerations:** Expertise is required due to its proximity to the brachial artery and nerves and its deeper location than the basilic vein.

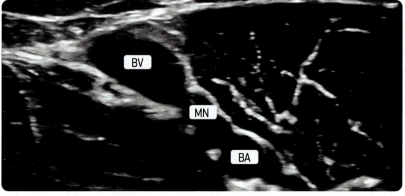

Fig-3-22. The brachial vein (BV) is found alongside the brachial artery (BA) and the median nerve (MN).

Median cubital vein

- **Location:** Found in the antecubital fossa, the area on the anterior side of the elbow.
- **Advantages:** Prominent and easily accessible for drawing blood and IV access.
- **Considerations:** Less suitable for long-term IVs because its location at the elbow flexion point poses a risk of occlusion and dislodgement.

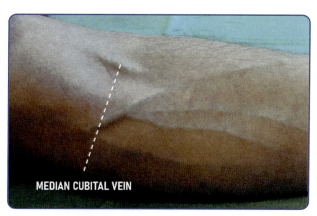

Fig-3-23. The median cubital vein is found in the antecubital fossa and is easily accessible for drawing blood or IV access.

Median antebrachial vein

- **Location:** Found in the midline of the anterior aspect of the forearm.
- **Advantages:** Ideal for short-term IV therapies.
- **Considerations:** Avoid bifurcations into the median cephalic and median basilic veins during insertion.

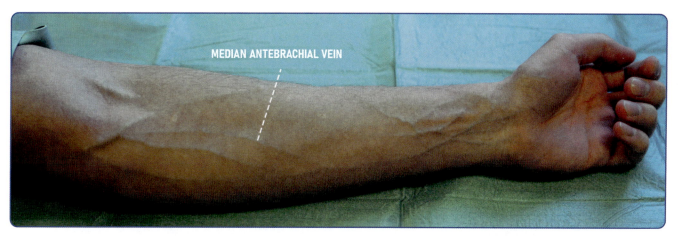

Fig-3-24. The median antebrachial vein is found in the midline of the anterior aspect of the forearm and is ideal for short-term IV therapies.

Cephalic vein

- **Location:** Starts at the radial aspect of the dorsal venous network of the hand and runs on the lateral side of the arm to the shoulder.
- **Advantages:** Surface position on the arm allows easier access.
- **Considerations:** Location near the wrist may be challenging due to the depth of the vein here.

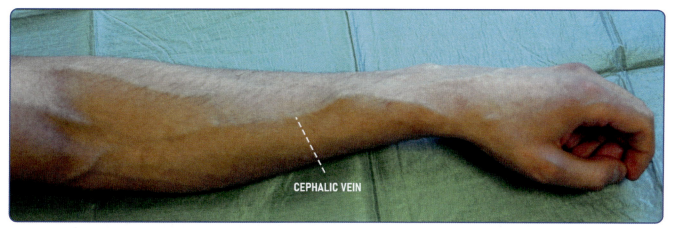

Fig-3-25. The cephalic vein starts at the radial aspect of the dorsal venous network and runs on the lateral side of the arm.

03 Anatomy of the vein and the venous system

Basilic vein

- **Location:** Starts on the ulnar side of the dorsal venous network of the hand and runs on the medial side of the arm.
- **Advantages:** Larger diameter often provides good blood flow for IV therapies, and this vein is isolated from arteries and nerves.
- **Considerations:** Deeper than the cephalic vein, requiring skilled catheter placement.

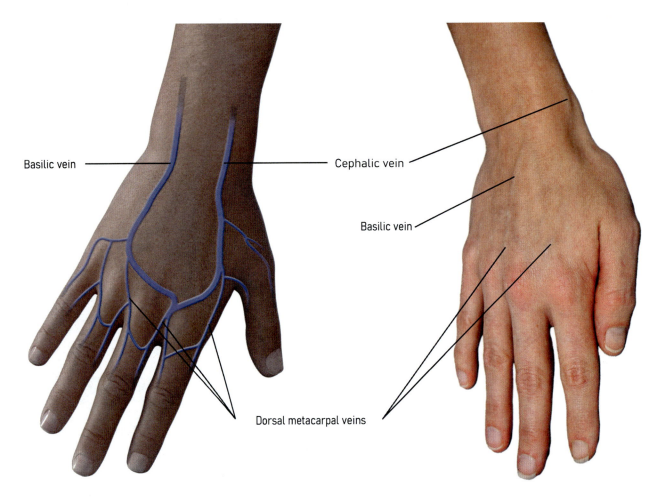

Fig-3-26. The cephalic, basilic, and dorsal metacarpal veins are excellent choices for insertion sites for peripheral venous catheters.

Dorsal metacarpal veins

- **Location:** Dorsal side of the hand, across the metacarpal bones.
- **Advantages:** Easily accessible and visible in most patients.
- **Considerations:**
    - Can be accidentally dislodged due to hand movement.
    - Potentially more painful site for patients.
    - Veins may roll easily, so have the patient make a fist for IV access.
    - Inconvenient location, restricts the use of the hand.

Access the videos for this section by scanning the QR code at the beginning of the chapter.

Commonly used sites for IV cannulation in the upper extremity

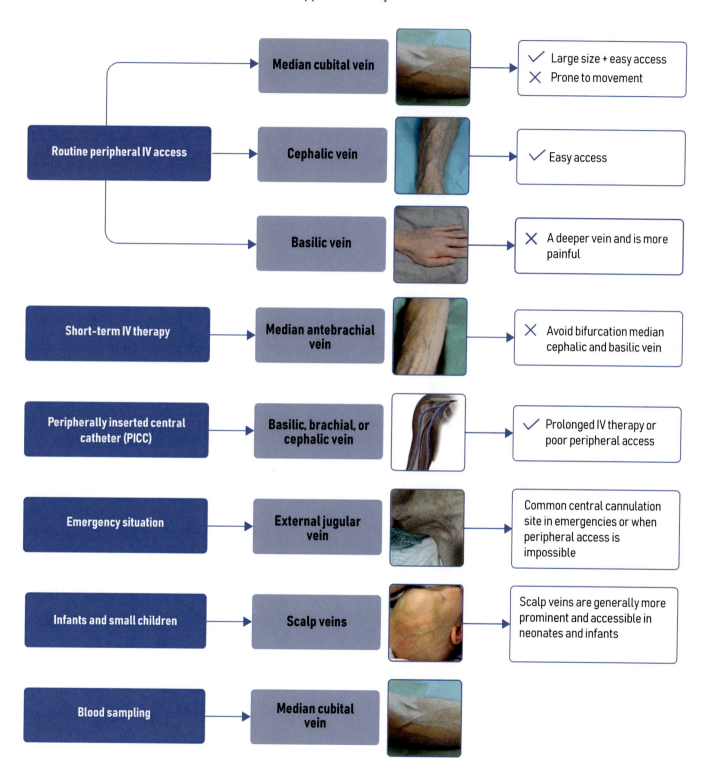

Fig-3-27. Commonly used sites for IV cannulations in the upper extremity and the rationale for their selection.

For peripheral IV access, veins in the upper extremities are often chosen due to their easy access (and reduced risk of complications). When selecting a site for IV cannulation, factors like the patient's age, health condition, and the purpose of the IV therapy are important. It's crucial to avoid areas near joints or where the body bends to limit catheter movement and lower the chances of the catheter coming out or fluid leaking into the tissue. Additionally, consider the comfort of the patient and the likelihood of complications at each site.

> **TIPS**
> - Ask the patient about their past IV or blood draw experiences.
> - Find out which veins worked well and which didn't.
> - Avoid veins they had difficulty with in the past to reduce anxiety and complications.

Lower extremity

Peripheral venous catheter insertion in the lower extremity is generally reserved when upper extremity sites are unavailable, contraindicated, or for pediatric patients. Here are some recommendations for choosing a vein in the lower extremity.

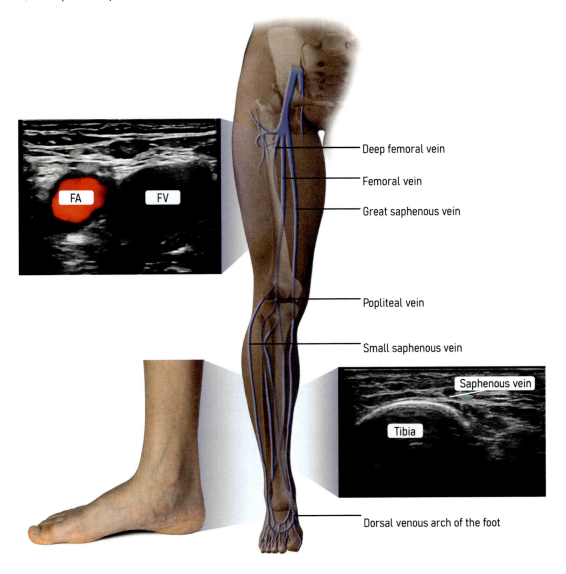

Fig-3-28. Insertion sites for peripheral catheter placement in the lower extremity. FA, femoral artery; FV, femoral vein.

Femoral vein (for large catheters)

- **Location:** Runs alongside the femoral artery in the upper thigh and groin area.
- **Advantages:** Can accommodate larger catheters, including central venous lines.
- **Considerations:** Increased infection and thrombosis risk. It lies close to the femoral artery, requiring caution to avoid unintentional arterial puncture.

Great saphenous vein

- **Location:** The longest vein in the body, running along the length of the leg. It originates from where the dorsal vein of the big toe (hallux) merges with the dorsal venous arch of the foot and extends up the medial aspect of the leg and thigh, ultimately draining into the femoral vein in the groin area. For IV cannulation, the great saphenous vein is usually found just medial to the medial malleolus of the ankle. The medial malleolus is the prominence on the inner side of the ankle, formed by the lower end of the tibia bone.
- **Clinical facts:** Its superficial location makes it accessible for various medical procedures, including venous access for long-term treatments, and harvesting for bypass surgery.
- **Risk of injury:** Due to its superficial path, the great saphenous vein is susceptible to injury, which can lead to complications such as inflammation or varicose veins.
- **Assessment:** The area near the medial malleolus should be examined for signs of venous insufficiency, such as swelling, skin changes, or the presence of varicose veins, which can preclude its use for cannulation and IV access in some situations.
- **Advantages:** Multiple access points are possible, being the longest vein in the body.
- **Considerations:** Thrombophlebitis and infection risks, especially near the groin.

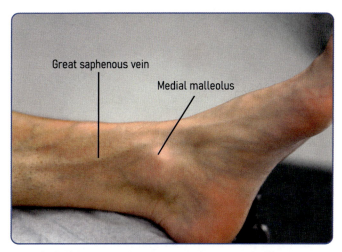

Fig-3-29. The great saphenous vein in the lower extremity. The vein is usually found just medial to the medial malleolus of the ankle.

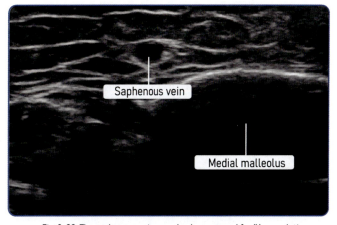

Fig-3-30. The saphenous vein can also be accessed for IV cannulation with ultrasound guidance.

Lesser (small) saphenous vein

- **Location:** The lesser saphenous vein is a superficial vein located in the posterior aspect of the leg. Unlike the great saphenous vein, which runs along the medial side of the leg, the lesser saphenous vein follows a path along the back of the leg. It starts at the lateral side of the dorsal venous arch of the foot, runs along the posterior calf, and joins the popliteal vein.
- **Advantages:** Accessibility, especially in the calf region.
- **Considerations:** As with the great saphenous vein, there is a greater risk of thrombophlebitis.

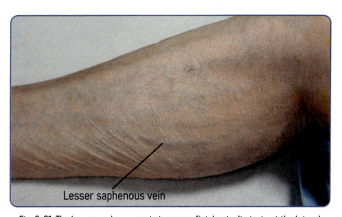

Fig-3-31. The lesser saphenous vein is a superficial vein. It starts at the lateral side of the dorsal venous arch and runs along the posterior calf.

Dorsal venous arch of the foot

- **Location:** Dorsal aspect of the foot.
- **Advantages:** Surface accessibility. Small veins that can easily be cannulated.
- **Considerations:** Commonly used in emergencies. However, it is prone to infection and accidental dislodgement due to movement and weight-bearing. It is suitable only for small gauge IV catheters.

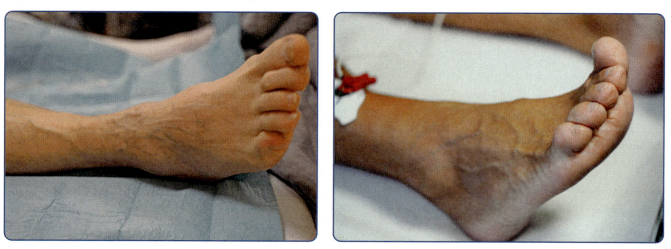

Fig-3-32. The dorsal venous arch of the foot is a potential insertion site for a peripheral venous catheter.

Commonly used sites for IV cannulation in the lower extremity

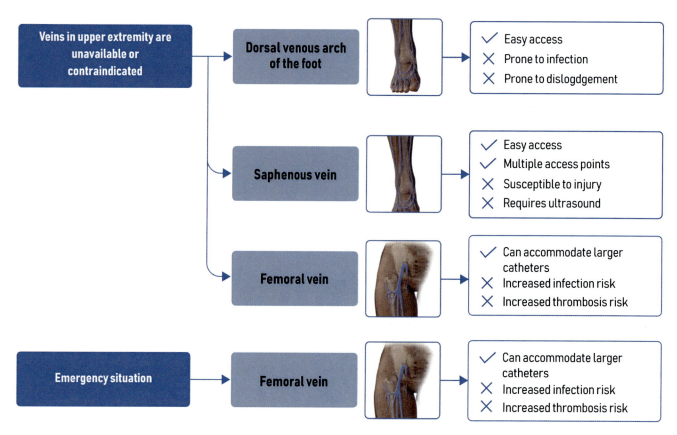

Fig-3-33. Commonly used sites for IV cannulations in the lower extremity and the practical considerations for their selection.

Adult patients

In adults, the veins of the lower extremities are typically considered as alternative sites for IV access only when upper extremity sites are unavailable or unsuitable. This is because there is a greater risk of complications associated with lower extremity venous access, such as:

- **Deep vein thrombosis (DVT):** The risk of developing DVT is significantly higher in the veins of the lower extremities compared to those in the upper extremities. This risk is even greater in patients with certain conditions, such as diabetes or peripheral vascular disease, which affect blood flow and vessel integrity.
- **Infection:** The risk of catheter-related infection is also elevated with lower extremity IV access, partly due to the difficulty in maintaining optimal hygiene and aseptic technique in these areas.
- **Phlebitis:** Inflammation of the veins is more common in the lower extremities, potentially leading to discomfort, swelling, and complications in drug delivery. One of the contributing factors is gravity-related venostasis.

Given these risks, when lower extremity veins are used for IV cannulation, it's important to employ meticulous hygiene practices, adhere strictly to aseptic techniques, and conduct regular assessments of the catheter site to identify and manage complications early.

Pediatric patients

In contrast to adults, the veins in the lower extremities are more commonly utilized for IV access in pediatric patients. This difference is partly due to the challenges of securing IV access in the smaller and more delicate veins of the upper extremities in children.

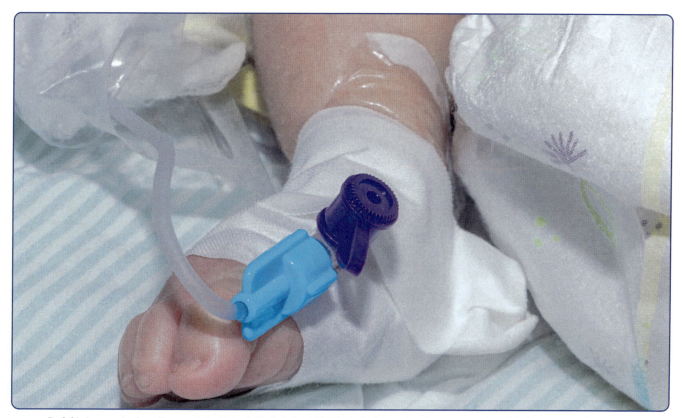

Fig 3-34. An example of a well-secured IV catheter in the foot of a child. Veins in the lower extremity are commonly used for IV access in pediatric patients.

Pediatric patients generally have a lower risk of DVT associated with lower extremity IV access compared to adults. However, this does not eliminate the need for vigilance:

- **Continuous monitoring:** Regular monitoring of the IV site is essential to promptly detect signs of infiltration, infection, or other complications. This is particularly important in pediatric patients who may not be able to communicate discomfort or pain as clearly as adults.
- **Hygiene and technique:** As with adults, maintaining strict hygiene and aseptic insertion techniques is vital to minimize infection risks.

Site selection criteria

The decision to use lower extremity veins for IV access should be guided by these criteria:

- **Clinical scenario:** The nature and urgency of the IV access.
- **Anticipated duration of therapy:** Short or long-term use.
- **Type of infusion:** Certain medications or solutions may be more irritating to veins, requiring careful consideration of the most appropriate site for administration to reduce the risk of complications.

Conclusion

Selecting the optimal site for peripheral venous catheter insertion, especially in the lower extremities, requires a carefully balancing the clinical need, patient-specific factors, and the potential risks and benefits. Adherence to best practices in catheter insertion and management is essential to minimize complications, ensure the safety and comfort of the patient, and achieve successful therapeutic outcomes.

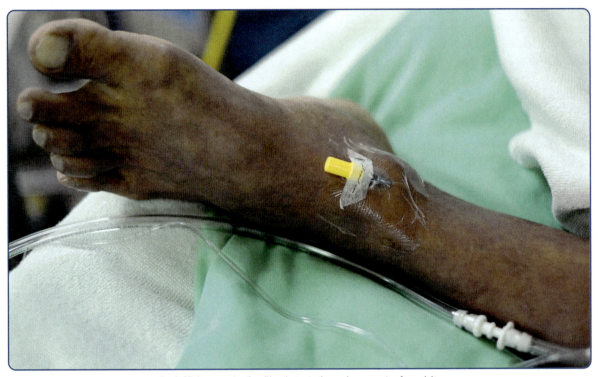

Fig 3-35. An example of an IV catheter in the saphenous vein of an adult.

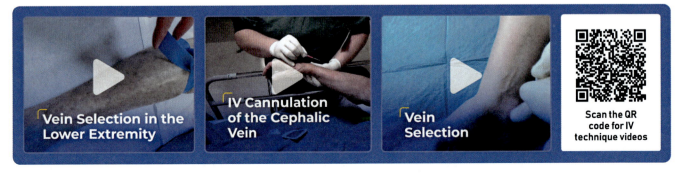

04

Scan the QR code for IV technique videos

MASTERING THE TECHNIQUE OF PERIPHERAL IV CATHETERIZATION

The insertion of a peripheral IV catheter is a routine procedure in medical practice. This chapter provides practical guidance on the insertion of IV catheters, and it primarily focuses on the insertion of IV catheters in the arms or the back of the hand. These sites are preferred due to their accessibility and abundant suitable veins. For techniques and considerations regarding IV access in other, less common anatomical sites, please refer to *Chapter 6: IV catheterization in less common anatomical sites* and *Chapter 10: IV catheterization in the central venous system.*

While reading through this chapter, remember that this guide provides a standard procedure protocol: different patients and healthcare settings may require deviation from the protocols provided here. Likewise, medical professionals should ensure they comply with patient safety and infectious guidelines.

4.1 Getting ready: Steps to take before the IV cannulation

Patient identification and preparation

- Introduce yourself to the patient.
- Confirm the patient's identity using the appropriate hospital protocol (checklist).
- Explain the procedure to the patient: Why, how, and where.
- Obtain informed consent if not covered elsewhere.

Scan the QR code for IV technique videos

Have the equipment ready

Before initiating IV access, prepare by gathering all necessary equipment and ensuring it's readily accessible. The preparation is key to facilitating a smooth IV cannulation process and preventing potential difficulties that could arise during the procedure. Having everything at hand increases efficiency and enhances patient comfort and safety by minimizing delays and the need for repeated attempts.

Here's a list of what is typically needed for IV cannulation:

- **Tourniquet:** Results in venostasis and makes veins more prominent.
- **Transparent dressing or adhesive bandage:** Secures the IV cannula after insertion.
- **Sterile gauze or cotton balls:** Useful for applying pressure post cannulation or if the attempt is unsuccessful.
- **IV catheter:** Typically, over-the-needle design. Available in various sizes to match specific clinical needs and the patient's vein size.
- **Sharps container:** A dedicated space for disposing of used needles.
- **Antiseptic solution:** Needed for skin disinfection (typically: alcohol, chlorhexidine, or povidone-iodine).
- **Gloves:** Maintain an aseptic technique for the patient's and your safety.
- **Extension tubing:** A flexible connection to the main IV after the cannulation.
- **Saline flush/syringe:** Occasionally used to test the IV and detect paravenous injection.

Fig-4-36. The equipment needed to insert a peripheral IV catheter. A) A tourniquet. B) Transparent dressing or adhesive bandage. C) Sterile gauze. D) IV catheter. E) Sharps container. F) Antiseptic solution. G) Sterile or non-sterile gloves.

Optional equipment

- **Local or topical anesthetic (commonly used for children):**
  - Injectable 1% lidocaine without epinephrine.
  - A cream or gel with various mixtures of lidocaine, tetracaine, or prilocaine.
- **Immobilization board:** Utilized when inserting a catheter over a joint to maintain stability and safety during the procedure.

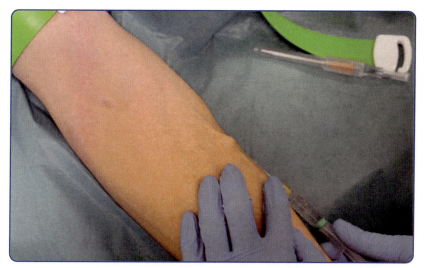

Fig-4-37. Local anesthetic infiltration with 1% lidocaine subcutaneously can be used to decrease the discomfort during insertion of a large-bore IV.

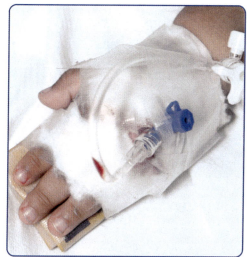

Fig-4-38. Immobilization board to maintain stability and safety during IV insertion.

Additional considerations

- **Chlorhexidine hypersensitivity:** In patients with a history of sensitivity to chlorhexidine, opt for an alternative skin disinfectant to avoid allergic reactions.
- **Latex allergy:** Use latex-free gloves and tourniquets.
- **Sterile field:** Typically unnecessary for peripheral venous cannulation. Regardless, always adhere to aseptic, no-touch techniques.

Catheter-securement devices

IV catheter-securing devices play a critical role in medical care by ensuring that IV catheters remain in place to deliver fluids and medications or to draw blood. These devices are designed to reduce the risk of catheter-related complications, such as dislodgement or infection. Various designs are available, including adhesive tapes, suture-based devices, and advanced adhesive dressings. Each type offers unique benefits, catering to different patient needs and clinical situations. For instance, adhesive dressings are often preferred for their ease of use and comfort, while suture-based devices may be used in situations requiring a more secure attachment. The choice of an IV catheter-securing device should consider factors such as the duration of IV therapy, patient activity level, and skin sensitivity. Proper selection and application of these devices are essential for enhancing patient comfort, minimizing complications, and ensuring the effective delivery of IV therapies.

Additionally, several securing devices are available also to secure the IV tubing, providing an additional layer of protection against accidental catheter dislodgement.

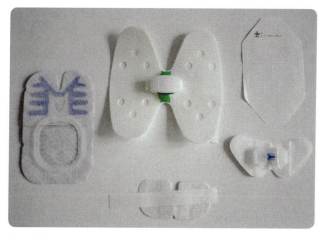

Fig-4-39. Examples of different types of catheter securing systems that can be used to tape down the IV catheter.

04 Mastering the technique of peripheral IV catheterization

IV starter kits

An IV starter kit is a pre-packaged sterile set containing all essential tools for inserting a peripheral IV.

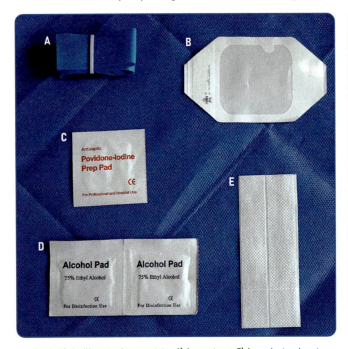

Fig-4-40. An IV starter kit containing A) A tourniquet. B) An occlusive dressing. C) A povidone-iodine pad to disinfect. D) Two alcohol pads to disinfect. E) A catheter-securing device.

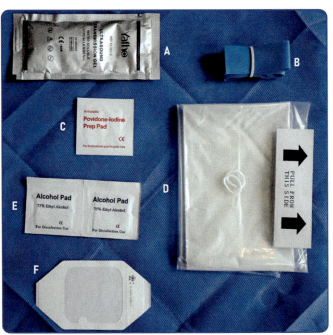

Fig-4-41. An IV starter kit containing all suplies for ultrasound-guided IV cannulations. A) Ultrasound gel. B) A tourniquet. C) A povidone-iodine pad to disinfect. D) A probe cover with two elastic bands to secure the probe cover. E) Two alcohol pads to disinfect. F) An occlusive dressing to secure the catheter.

Select the best cannula size

- Choose the smallest gauge for the planned IV flow rate needed for the prescribed IV therapy. This helps minimize injury to the vein and patient discomfort. Use common sense in selection - the larger the gauge of the catheter - the more risk for vein thrombosis and inflammation.
- The type and viscosity of the fluid or medication to be administered are important for the selection of the catheter gauge size and site for venous access. The higher viscosity of the IV fluids and injectables that cause vein irritation requires a larger IV cannula gauge and larger veins.
- 18G or 20G IV cannulas are most commonly used for routine infusions in adults (14G or 16G for high-volume infusions).
- 22G or 24G IV cannulas are more suitable for infants and small children.

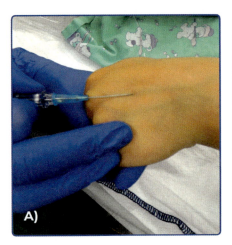
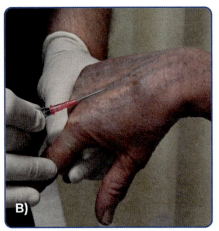
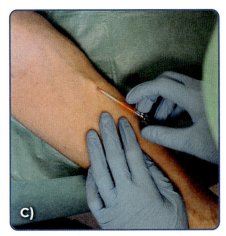

Fig-4-42. 22G (blue) (A) is used for pediatric patients. 20G (pink) (B) is used most commonly for routine infusions in adults. 14G (orange) (C) is used for large vein cannulation.

Hand hygiene and gloves

Hand hygiene and the use of gloves are important in ensuring the safety and effectiveness of IV cannulations. Washing hands thoroughly with soap and water or using an alcohol-based hand rub removes potentially harmful microorganisms that could be introduced into the patient's bloodstream during the procedure. Wearing sterile or non-sterile gloves creates a barrier between the healthcare provider's hands and the patient, reducing the risk of contaminating the IV site. Gloves protect the patient and healthcare provider by preventing cross-contamination from touching non-sterile surfaces or equipment before cannulation. Hand hygiene and gloves are fundamental components of infection control practices in healthcare settings, significantly lowering the incidence of catheter-related bloodstream infections and enhancing patient outcomes.

Fig-4-43. Use sterile or non-sterile, disposable gloves to maintain an aseptic technique throughout the procedure.

DO NOT FORGET:
- Wash hands using soap and water or an alcohol-based hand rub.
- Use sterile or non-sterile, disposable gloves to maintain an aseptic technique throughout the procedure.

4.2 The art and technique of IV catheter insertion

IV catheter insertion is both an art and a technique, reflecting the skill and expertise required to master this procedure. It demands technical proficiency and a nuanced understanding of patient anatomy and vein selection. The development of this skill set is a specialized process, necessitating focused practice and experience to achieve proficiency. This combination of artistry and technique is essential for effectively and efficiently placing IV catheters, a critical component in patient care, as the Germans would say: "Fingerspitzengefühl." We strongly recommend practicing the skill regularly in a simulator to develop the feel and technique that can be transposed to patient care (see *Chapter 11.1: IV access simulators*).

Patient position
While the ideal position varies for different insertion sites, here are a few basics to remember:
- Place the patient in a comfortable position to optimize the exposure of the insertion site.
- Position the extremity being cannulated on a comfortable surface.
- Position the insertion site below the level of the heart to maximize blood pooling and enlarge the veins.
- Make all supplies and equipment easily accessible on a nearby tray.
- Use a clean, organized tray for equipment.

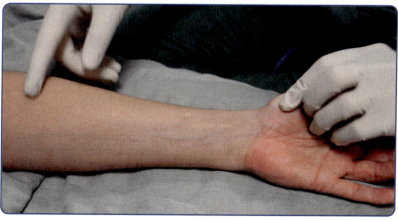

Fig-4-44. Place the patient in a comfortable position to optimize the exposure of the insertion site.

The technique and fine art of tourniquet tightening

What is a tourniquet?

The use of a tourniquet during venous cannulation serves several important purposes that facilitate the successful placement of a venous catheter:

1. Vein engorgement

The primary purpose of a tourniquet is to temporarily restrict venous blood flow back to the heart without impeding arterial blood flow to the limb. This causes veins to fill with blood and become more engorged, making them easier to visualize and palpate. The increased visibility and prominence of the veins significantly aid in identifying suitable veins for cannulation.

2. Improved accuracy

By making the veins more prominent, a tourniquet reduces the number of attempts needed to successfully cannulate a vein. This is particularly helpful in patients with difficult venous access, such as those with small, fragile, or deeply situated veins.

3. Correct application

Apply the tourniquet snugly enough to engorge the veins but not so tight as to cause pain or completely obstruct arterial blood flow.

4. Time limit

The tourniquet should not be left in place for more than a few minutes to prevent discomfort and potential complications. Prolonged application can lead to patient discomfort, tissue damage, or inaccurate lab results if blood is drawn.

5. Location

It's typically placed a few inches above the venipuncture site, on the upper arm for forearm veins, or on the forearm for wrist and hand veins.

In summary, a tourniquet is a crucial tool in venous cannulation, serving to enhance vein visibility and palpability, which in turn improves the ease and success of the procedure, reduces patient discomfort, and minimizes the risk of complications.

> **Access the videos for this section by scanning the QR code at the beginning of the chapter.**

Apply the tourniquet

- Position the tourniquet around the extremity, approximately 5-10 cm (2-4 inches) above the intended puncture site.
- When accessing veins on the hand, apply the tourniquet either on the arm or the forearm.
- Ensure the tourniquet lays flat against the skin and remains untwisted for optimal performance. A twisted tourniquet is less effective and uncomfortable for the patient.

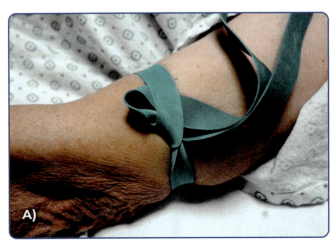 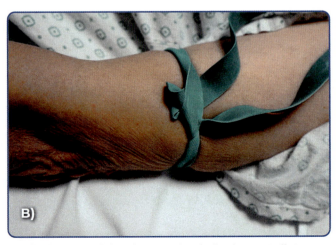

Fig-4-45. A) Correct tourniquet application. B) A twisted tourniquet, which is less effective in accomplishing the venostasis and vein enlargement effect.

The design of tourniquets used for IV access and phlebotomy influences the technique of application and tightening. While the specific method may vary depending on the tourniquet's design, there are general guidelines to follow:

- **Appropriate tightness:** Ensure the tourniquet is applied snugly enough to restrict venous flow without impeding arterial circulation.
- **Correct placement:** Position the tourniquet close to the venipuncture site but not so close as to interfere with the procedure.
- **Knowledge of tourniquet types:** Be familiar with the various types of tourniquets available and understand the nuances of each design to optimize venous access and ensure patient comfort and safety.
- **Application technique:** Grasp one end of the tourniquet and pull the other end using the opposite hand.
- **Secure fastening:** Tie or fasten the tourniquet securely using a self-adhesive end or buckle if available.
- **Vein identification:** Look for distended veins below the level of the tourniquet.
- **Vein palpation:** Gently feel the veins to ensure they are more prominent and filled with blood.
- **Patient comfort:** Ask the patient if they are experiencing excessive discomfort or pain; a too-tight tourniquet may cause pain or harm underlying tissues.

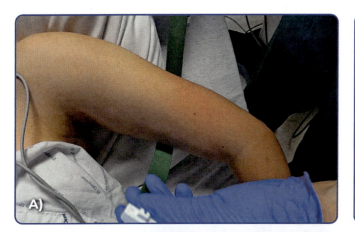
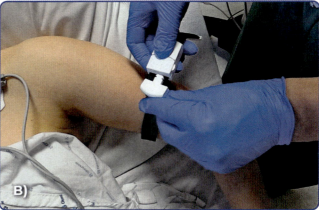
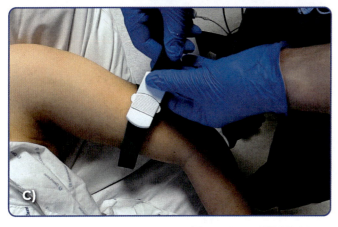
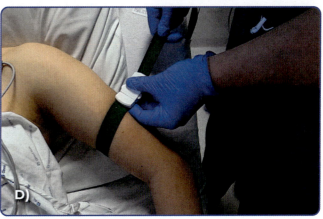

Fig-4-46. Tourniquet application steps: A) Expose the arm WITHOUT elevating it (elevation empties the blood from the extremity). B) Secure the tourniquet. C) and D) Tighten to the patient's tolerance.

TIPS

- **Be patient:** Give the veins time to properly fill when using a tourniquet, especially in dehydrated patients (a few minutes).
- **Consider using multiple tourniquets:** Use a second or third tourniquet to help the veins fill with blood in patients with difficult access.
- **Patients can also help:** Ask the patient to open and close the hand repeatedly (making a fist). This activates the muscle pump and draws more blood into the veins, facilitating vein recognition and IV access.

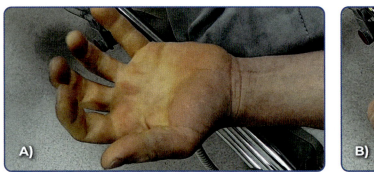
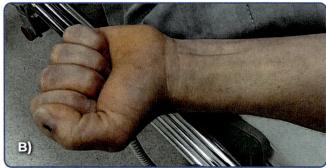

Fig-4-47. Ask the patient to open (A) and close (B) the hand repeatedly to encourage blood flow into the veins and to facilitate vein recognition.

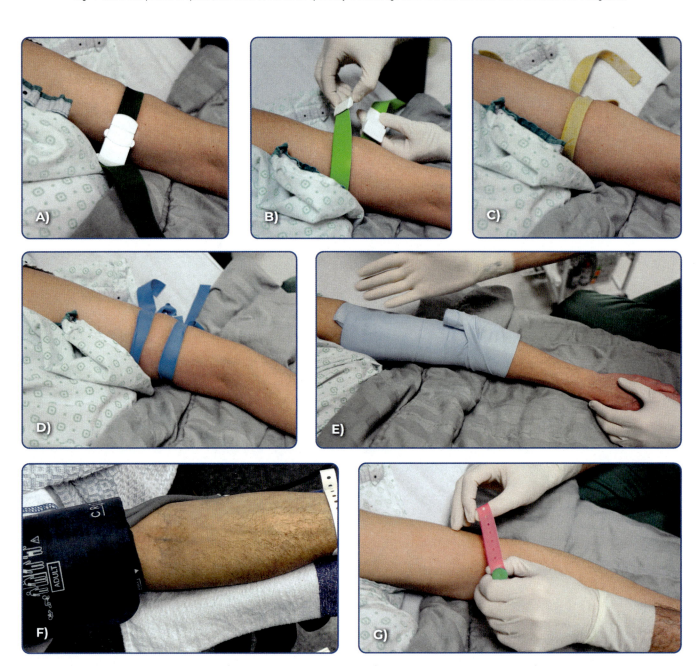

Fig-4-48: Several tourniquet designs are available. A) A tourniquet with a buckle system. B) A tourniquet with a magnetic closing. C) A rubber band used as a tourniquet. D) The use of two parallel rubber tourniquets to encourage blood flow to the superficial veins. E) A rubber band (Esmarch, 10-15 cm or 4-6 inches in width) wrapped around the upper arm and forearm to encourage blood flow to the superficial veins. F) Using a blood pressure cuff as a tourniquet during venipuncture. G) Smaller more distensible tourniquets are available for pediatric patients to prevent blocking the arterial blood flow.

Choose the perfect spot: guide to vein selection

Selecting the ideal vein for IV insertion is a skill that healthcare professionals develop with experience. Whether you opt for upper or lower extremity vein cannulation, it's essential to follow these fundamental guidelines:

- **Straight veins are the best:** Select a straight vein to facilitate easier needle entry, whenever possible.
- **Superficial veins are easier than deeper veins:** Choose veins closer to the skin's surface for easier access.
- **Avoid branching veins:** Choose veins that do not branch out to avoid complications near venous valves, which are often located near these branches.

Fig-4-49. Vein selection. Healthy veins feel bouncy and refill when depressed.

- **Visibility:** Look for blue or darkened lines under the skin. Veins may appear more prominently in fair-skinned individuals.
- **Palpability:** Gently feel the veins using the index or middle finger. This is important, especially for patients in whom veins are not be visible.

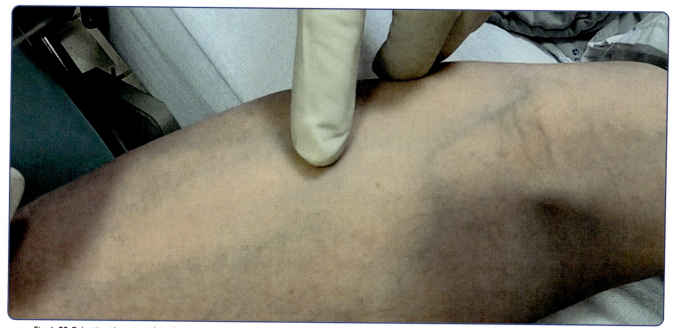

Fig-4-50. Palpating the veins of the forearm to select the perfect vein. If a vein feels round and springy, even if not visible, it is likely suitable for cannulation.

04 Mastering the technique of peripheral IV catheterization

- **Turgor and elasticity:** Healthy veins feel bouncy and quickly refill when depressed. These are generally good choices for IV placement.
- **Size:** Larger veins can hold larger catheters and are less likely to collapse during IV insertion.
- **Start distally:** Start at the dorsal metacarpal veins and work proximally (i.e., cephalic, basilic, radial, and median cubital veins) if needed.
- **Avoid:**
    - Areas of joint flexion as they can increase the risk of the catheter becoming dislodged or kinked.
    - Veins that feel hard or cord-like (they may be thrombosed).
    - Veins in an extremity with a known blood clot, an AV fistula or graft, mastectomy, or lymph node dissection.
    - Sites that are inflamed, infected, or have extensive scarring.
    - Inserting an IV distal to a previous infiltration or phlebitis site.

> **TIPS**
> - **Trust the feel:** If a vein feels round and springy, even if not visible, it is likely suitable for cannulation. However, veins that feel hard do not appear to empty when pressed and are likely thrombosed and unsuitable for cannulation.
> - **Use alcohol wipes:** This helps enlarge veins and can change the skin's reflection, making veins more noticeable. This technique may be useful, especially in patients with darker skin.

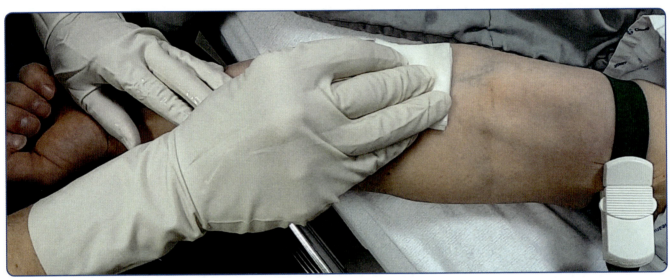

Fig-4-51. Use alcohol wipes to visualize the veins more easily.

> **The application of alcohol on the skin can enhance the visibility of veins** aiding in venous cannulation.
> Here are some mechanisms:
>
> 1. **Vasodilation**
> Alcohol causes peripheral vasodilation, where blood vessels near the surface of the skin engorge. This increases blood flow to the area, making the veins more prominent and easier to identify and access. The cooling effect of alcohol as it evaporates from the skin can also stimulate reflex vasodilation as the body attempts to regulate temperature.
>
> 2. **Skin disinfection and contrast**
> Alcohol acts as a disinfectant, cleaning the skin's surface, which can improve the contrast between the skin and the veins beneath it. By removing dirt, oils, and natural skin flora, the skin becomes more apparent and the veins can appear more defined against the skin's surface.
>
> 3. **Tightening of the skin**
> The astringent properties of alcohol can cause the skin to tighten slightly, reducing surface area and potentially making underlying structures like veins appear more superficial. This effect can help in making the veins more palpable and easier to access with a needle.

Proper insertion site disinfection

Maintaining an aseptic technique and proper hygiene is essential to minimize the infection risk.

Choice of antiseptic

- **Alcohol:** Probably the most common disinfectant used for IV cannulation. Often used in combination with other antiseptics, alcohol is effective against many bacteria and viruses.
- **Chlorhexidine gluconate (CHG):** This antiseptic provides rapid and persistent antimicrobial action and is effective against a broad spectrum of microorganisms.
- **Iodine-based solutions (povidone-iodine):** Another commonly used antiseptic, especially if there's a contraindication for CHG.

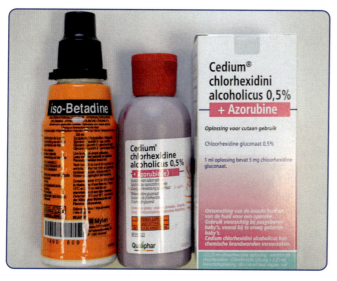

Fig-4-52. Different antiseptic solutions to disinfect the insertion site.

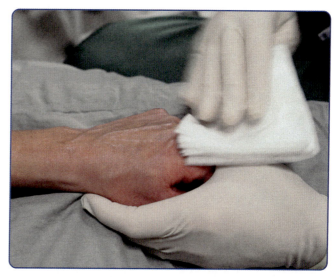

Fig-4-53. Alcohol wipes are used to disinfect the insertion site before IV cannulation.

Asepsis

- Before catheter insertion, ensure the skin is clean and free from debris. Use an antiseptic, applying it in a circular motion beginning at the insertion point and moving outward. This effectively disinfects the area.
- Let the antiseptic airdry completely before inserting the catheter to eliminate bacteria and prevent antiseptic residue from entering the skin (painful).
- Always check for patient allergies to specific antiseptics before using them.
- Once the site is disinfected, avoid touching it. If there's a need to re-examine the vein's position, remember that any contact requires re-disinfection.
- After insertion, maintain cleanliness at the site.

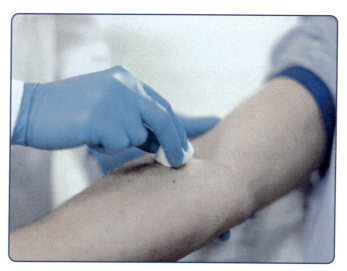

Fig-4-54. Disinfection of the insertion site. You can use either prepared alcohol wipes, povidone-iodine, or multiuse antiseptic.

Access the videos for this section by scanning the QR code at the beginning of the chapter.

Hold it steady: ensuring vein stability

During IV catheter insertion, stabilizing ("fixing") the vein is vital for a successful venipuncture and to minimize trauma to the vein and surrounding tissue by repeated failed attempts. Here's an overview of techniques and considerations to ensure vein stability during venipuncture or IV cannulation:

- **Superficial veins:** These veins are not firmly anchored by the connective tissue and tend to roll away. After investing time in identifying and selecting the most suitable vein, it would be frustrating to see it shift ("roll") just as you begin the IV insertion. To prevent this, using **"counter traction"** during insertion can be a game-changer.
- **Deeper veins:** In contrast, deeper veins benefit from the stability provided by the surrounding connective tissue. Test the vein's stability by nudging it from side to side. If it stands firm without moving, counter traction might not be necessary.

Identified a suitable superficial vein for insertion?

- **Use the counter traction technique to stabilize the vein:** Place the thumb of the non-dominant hand a short distance below the selected insertion spot. Then, pull the skin gently distally.
- **Avoid this common mistake:** Stretching the skin away from the vein from both sides. It can also flatten it, reducing its size, palpability, and visibility, and making it more difficult to cannulate.

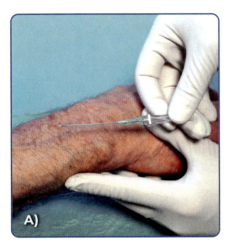
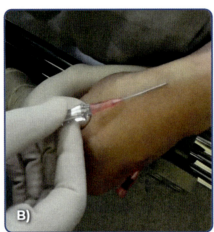
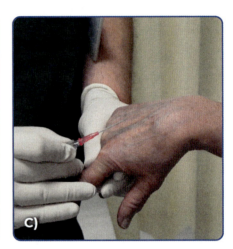

Fig-4-55. Examples of vein stabilization before the cannulation.

Use a low angle

When performing IV cannulation, be aware of the depth and position of the targeted vein to determine the needle insertion angle. Visualize the needle trajectory to ensure optimal needle angle direction. The objective is to insert and advance the catheter with the minimal angle necessary to reach the vein. Starting with a large angle to puncture the vein (common mistake), followed by re-adjustment of the angle, carries a risk of going through both walls of the vein and the subsequent failure.

Superficial veins

- Insert the needle at a shallow angle, typically between 10 to 30 degrees relative to the skin.
- Shallow veins that bulge out from the skin and travel across bones (i.e., dorsal veins of the hands, cephalic vein) require a very shallow angle of 15 degrees or less.

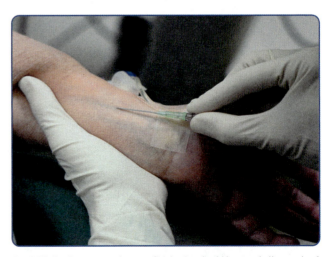

Fig-4-56. Needle insertion for superficial veins should be at a shallow angle of 10 to 30 degrees relative to the skin to avoid going through the posterior wall.

Deep veins

- Deeper veins (i.e., antecubital vein) require a slightly greater angle, (30-45 degrees).
- Once the skin is punctured, decrease the angle as the needle advances toward the vein.

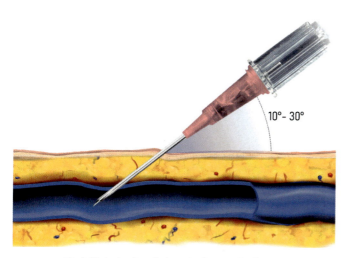

Fig-4-57. Angle of needle insertion for superficial veins.

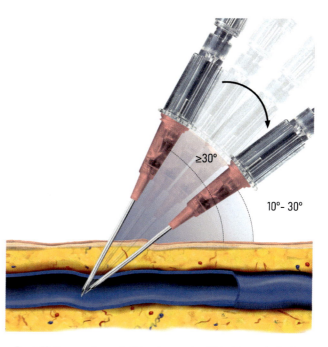

Fig-4-58. Decrease the angle. A too-steep angle will lead to puncturing the vein's back wall.

Nailing the needle insertion

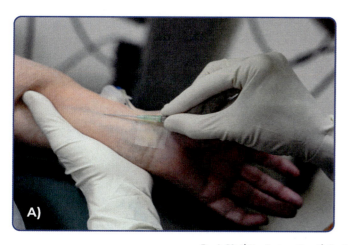

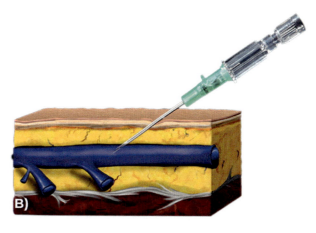

Fig-4-59. A) Needle insertion. B) Illustration of the needle insertion.

When inserting an IV catheter, here's a breakdown of the essential steps:

- Hold the needle securely with the dominant hand, either at the hub or using the grip pads.
- Make sure the needle bevel faces upward to facilitate the ease of vein entry and reduce the risk of skimming over the vein.
- Align the needle direction with the direction of the chosen vein.
- Let the patient know: "You might feel a little pinch when I start the IV."
- Insert the needle at a 10-30 degree angle to the skin about 1 to 2 cm (0.3-0.8 inches) distal to the intended point of vein entry.
- When there's limited space, and the IV needs to go right above the vein, start with a steeper angle for quick vein entry and then flatten the angle afterward.
- Steadily advance the needle.
- Anticipate a small "pop" or a loss of resistance, often felt as the needle enters the vein.
- The appearance of blood in the flashback chamber indicates the IV needle tip position.
- Advance the needle into the vein for approximately another 0.5-1 cm to ensure the catheter is also inside the vein, not just the needle tip.

- Stop advancing the needle-catheter system once sufficiently inside the vein, as going too deep can lead to the needle tip puncturing the vein's back wall and/or hematoma.
- Remember that in patients with thick-walled or sclerotic veins, a fast, deliberate insertion is helpful to penetrate the vein wall instead of pushing ("rolling") the vein away.

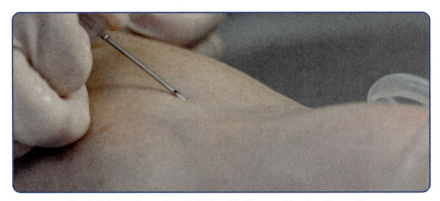

Fig-4-60. Insert the needle with the bevel facing upward to allow for smoother penetration into the vein.

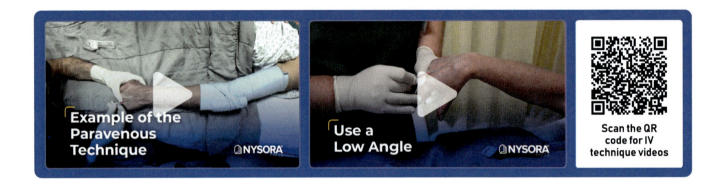

What should it feel like?

The secret of IV professionals is that they can feel the vein without seeing it, and they acquire a "feel" for when the needle enters the vein. While inserting the IV, resistance will be felt at two points. The initial resistance is met as the needle pierces through the patient's skin. The larger the needle, the greater the resistance. More force might be needed, especially in some (male) patients with thicker skin. Once the needle has passed through the skin, it enters the subcutaneous tissue with little to no resistance.

A subtle pop or moment of resistance will be felt, indicating entry into the vein. The blood flashback should be noticeable in the flashback chamber. The "pop" or "give" will be more perceptible in larger, healthy, or thick veins. This perception of entry into the vein is often the only clinical clue when inserting an IV in the dorsum of the hand in small children with difficult veins. The "pop" may be absent in small, delicate veins with thin walls.

Alternative approaches to vein cannulation

The most common or standard approach is the TOP approach, in which the needle is positioned and advanced directly over (above) the vein. However, a paravenous approach may sometimes be more appropriate.

Paravenous approach

- Position the needle at the vein's side, aiming along its path.
- Push the needle through the skin toward the vein.
- Keep the angle of the needle to the vein small to reduce the risk of puncturing the vein's opposite wall.
- Use this approach if the needle is accidentally inserted into the side of a vein or if the vein moves after insertion from the top.
- Once inside the vein, re-correct the angle of the needle to assume a parallell course to the vein.

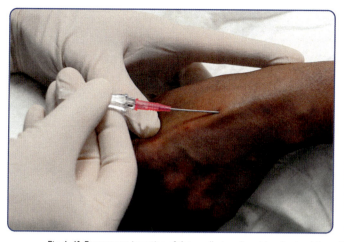 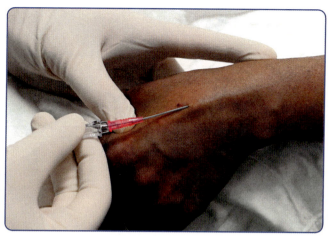

Fig-4-61. Paravenous insertion of the needle in a dorsal hand vein while maintaining a low angle to reduce the risk of puncturing the vein's opposite wall.

Insertion through a bifurcation

This approach may be appropriate to prevent vein rolling, and the bifurcation stabilizes the vein to be cannulated.

a. Insert the needle from the top above the bifurcation, aiming for needle entry slightly proximal to the bifurcation.
b. If the space allows, first insert the needle 1 cm below the bifurcation (better) and advance through the subcutaneous tissue into the vein through the bifurcation.
c. Another option is to insert the needle directly into the bifurcation. This can be advantageous in "rolling" veins, where the bifurcation stabilizes the vein at the point of entry.

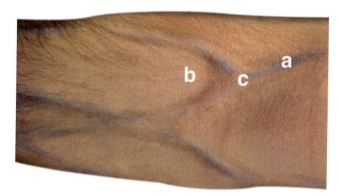

Fig-4-62. Example of a vein bifurcation and needle insertion strategies.

Look out for the blood flashback and advance the catheter

Blood appearing in the flashback chamber confirms the needle is inside the vein. However, this does not necessarily mean that the catheter is also in the vein, as the needle tip slightly precedes the catheter tip. Upon seeing the blood flashback, lower the angle so the needle becomes almost parallel to the body's surface, and advance another 0.5-1 cm to ensure both the needle and catheter are in the vein. Failing to adjust the angle may lead to a puncture of the vein's opposite wall when the needle is pushed further.

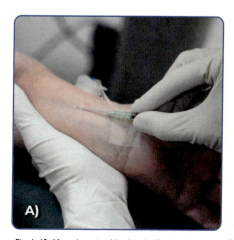 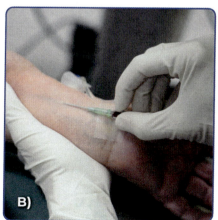 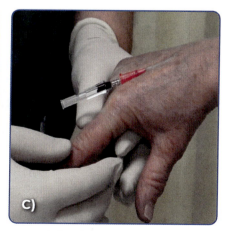

Fig-4-63. After observing blood in the flashback chamber (A), lower the angle of the needle and advance another 0.5-1 cm to ensure both needle and catheter are in the vein (B,C).

04 Mastering the technique of peripheral IV catheterization

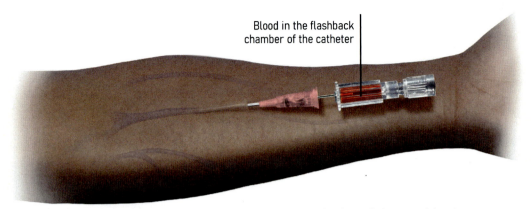

Fig-4-64. Illustration of blood in the flashback chamber, indicating that the needle has entered the vein.

After a blood flashback, advance the needle-catheter system an additional few millimeters to ensure the catheter is in the vein. Next, slide the catheter over the needle to its hub. The patient typically does not feel any discomfort during catheter advancement. If the patient complains of pain during the catheter sliding maneuver or if resistance is felt, the catheter may not be located in the vein.

> **TIPS**
>
> Larger catheters have more space between the needle tip and the catheter tip than smaller needles. This affects the depth at which the needle-catheter system needs to be advanced into the vein *after* obtaining the blood flashback.
>
> - **18G catheter:** Advance another 1-2 cm.
> - **22G and smaller catheters:** Advance another 0.5-1 cm.

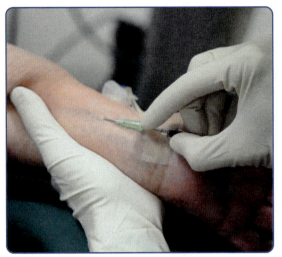

Fig-4-65. Thread the catheter over the needle into the vein.

4.3 Post-insertion procedure and catheter care

Retract the needle and attach the IV tubing

- After successful catheter placement, place the thumb above the insertion point to prevent blood leakage.
- Remove the needle.
- If needed, withdraw any blood for laboratory testing using a syringe or phlebotomy adapter.
- Attach the end of the IV tubing or the saline lock to the catheter hub.

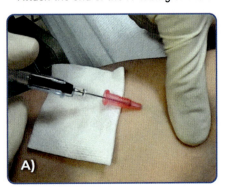
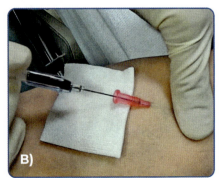
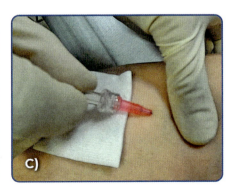

Fig-4-66. A) The thumb is placed above the insertion point to prevent blood leakage. B) Retract the needle. C) Attach the IV tubing to the catheter hub.

Release the tourniquet and secure the catheter

- Leave the tourniquet on until the cannulation's success is confirmed to maximize the benefits of the tourniquet to keeping the veins enlarged.
- Release the tourniquet.
- Start the infusion or flush the saline lock (inject about 5 mL of saline in rapid, small pulses).
- Fluid should flow freely. Check for any swelling or edema around the insertion site, which may indicate paravenous infusion.
- Wipe blood and fluid from the insertion site carefully to prevent accidentally dislodging the catheter.
- Cover the catheter with a transparent occlusive dressing.
- Use one of many different techniques and devices to secure the catheter and prevent its accidental dislodgement.
  - For example, if the design of the IV allows, loop the IV tubing and tape it to the skin away from the IV insertion site to prevent accidental traction on the tubing from dislodging the catheter.
- Apply an immobilization board as necessary.

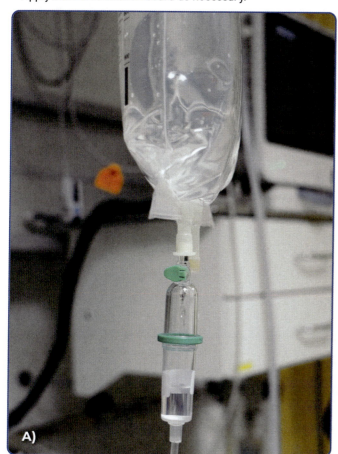
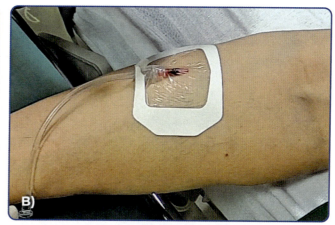
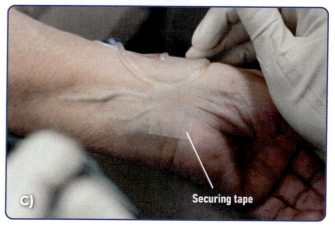

Fig-4-67. A) Check the IV flow. B) Secure the catheter with an occlusive dressing. C) Tape the tubing away from the IV insertion site to prevent dislodgement.

TIP
- Double-check that the tourniquet has been removed after securing the IV (common mistake).

Access the videos for this section by scanning the QR code at the beginning of the chapter.

4.4 Algorithm

Getting ready

PATIENT IDENTIFICATION AND PREPARATION

- Introduce yourself
- Confirm the patient's identity
- Explain the procedure
- Obtain informed consent
- Inform that cannulation may cause discomfort
- Rule out contraindications (e.g., ipsilateral breast cancer surgery, AV fistula).

GATHER SUPPLIES

- Gloves
- Tourniquet
- Antiseptic solution
- IV catheter
- Sterile gauze or cotton balls
- Extension tubing
- Transparent dressing or adhesive bandage

OPTIONAL EQUIPMENT

- Local or topical anesthetic (standard for children)
- Immobilization board
- Warm pack
- Saline flush/syringe
- Sharps container

ADDITIONAL CONSIDERATIONS

- Chlorhexidine hypersensitivity
- Latex hypersensitivity
- Sterile field
- Catheter placement

SELECT THE APPROPRIATE CANNULA SIZE

- Choose the smallest gauge for the intended indication
- Consider the type and viscosity of the fluid or medication to be administered
- Common sites (gauge)
  - **Adults:** 18-20G
  - **Infants:** 22-24G

HAND HYGIENE

- Use soap and water or alcohol-based hand rub
- Use gloves to maintain an aseptic technique

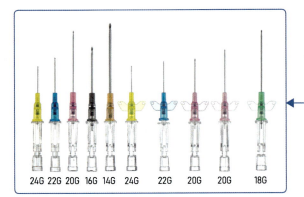

24G 22G 20G 16G 14G 24G   22G 20G 20G   18G

Catheter insertion

PATIENT POSITION

- Comfortable while exposing the insertion site
- Position the insertion site below the heart
- Ensure the ergonomics of the clinician
- Maintain a clean, secure, organized surface

TOURNIQUET TIGHTENING

- Apply the tourniquet 5-10 cm above the puncture site
- Tighten the tourniquet
- Look and feel for veins below the tourniquet

VEIN SELECTION

- Ideal vein is
  - Straight and visible
  - Close to the skin surface
  - Without valves
- Check for
  - Palpable veins
  - Elastic veins
  - Veins with a larger size
- Avoid
  - Areas of joint flexion
  - Veins that feel hard or cord-like
  - Veins with a known blood clot
  - Inflamed sites/extensive scarring
  - Site distal to a previous infiltration/with phlebitis
- Start distally

INSERTION SITE DISINFECTION

- Choice of antiseptic
  - Chlorhexidine gluconate
  - Iodine-based solutions
  - Alcohol
- Disinfect the site in an outward circular motion
- Allow the antiseptic to air dry completely
- Patients may be allergic to antiseptics
- Do not touch the cleaned site

ENSURING VEIN STABILITY

- **Superficial veins:** Use counter traction technique
- **Deeper veins:** Counter traction is probably not necessary as stability is provided by surrounding tissue
- Avoid stretching the skin away from the vein from both sides

NEEDLE ANGLE

- Aim to insert and advance the catheter as shallow as possible
- **Superficial veins**
  - Typically between 15-30° to the skin
  - Shallow veins that bulge out from the skin: ≤ 15°
- **Deep veins**
  - Typically between 30-45°
  - Decrease the angle once the skin is punctured and the needle advances toward the vein

NEEDLE INSERTION: STANDARD / TOP APPROACH

- Hold the needle securely with your dominant hand
- Face the needle bevel upward
- Align the needle above the chosen vein
- Insert the needle at a 15-30° angle and 1-2 cm distal to the insertion point
- Start with a sharper angle if you are right above the vein, and there is not enough space
- Steadily advance the needle
- Watch for blood in the flashback chamber and/or "pop" feeling
- Stop advancing the needle to prevent puncturing the back wall of the vein
- Use a fast, deliberate insertion to penetrate the vein wall in patients with thick or sclerotic veins

ALTERNATIVE APPROACHES

- Paravenous approach
- "Through a bifurcation approach"

ADVANCE THE CATHETER

- Blood in the flashback chamber means that the needle is inside the vein but the catheter may NOT
- Advance the needle an additional few mm in the vein to ensure that the catheter tip is also in the vein
- Slide the catheter over the needle into the vein

04 Mastering the technique of peripheral IV catheterization

Post-placement care

RETRACT THE NEEDLE

- Carefully retract the needle
- Hold the hub steady with the thumb
- Put the index finger over the insertion site to prevent blood leakage
- Attach the IV tubing or saline lock

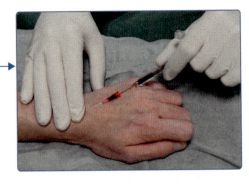

RELEASE THE TOURNIQUET

- Keep the tourniquet on until the catheter placement is verified
- Check the flow by starting the infusion or flushing the saline lock
- The fluid should flow freely
- Check for possible swelling or edema around the insertion site
- Wipe all blood and fluid from the insertion site
- Cover the catheter with an occlusive dressing
- Loop the IV tubing and tape it to the skin away from the insertion site
- Apply an immobilization board as necessary

FAILED INSERTION

- Do **NOT** take the failed IV catheter out; this may lead to hematoma formation and complicates potential retries at different sites: the catheter functions as a venous plug
- Keep the tourniquet on

TIP

- Always double-check that you removed the tourniquet before leaving the patient

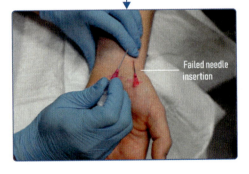

Failed needle insertion

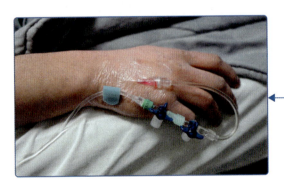

Scan the QR code for IV technique videos

05

Scan the QR code for IV technique videos

COMMON MISTAKES AND TROUBLESHOOTING

Understanding common mistakes and troubleshooting techniques in IV cannulation is crucial for enhancing success rates and ensuring patient safety. This knowledge prevents complications and empowers healthcare professionals to impart practical skills and insights to others, fostering a culture of continuous improvement and shared learning in clinical settings. Here's a rundown of what you should know.

5.1 Steering clear of common mistakes

This chapter focuses on identifying and correcting common mistakes during IV cannulation. By highlighting these errors, we aim to provide healthcare professionals with the insights needed to enhance their technique, reduce the risk of complications, and improve patient outcomes. This guidance is a foundation for novice and experienced practitioners to refine their skills, ensuring safer and more effective IV therapy.

Wrong choice of the catheter (A too-short catheter)

Mistake: Using a too-short catheter that only extends slightly into the vein is prone to dislodgement, particularly when the patient moves.

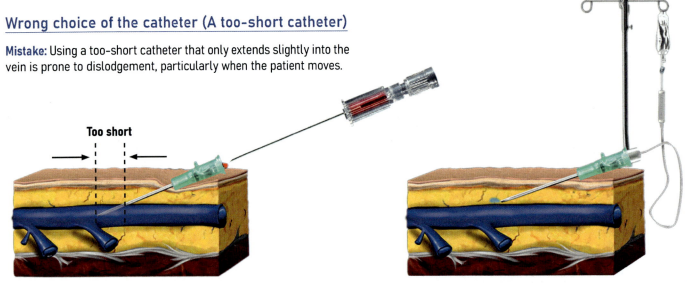

Fig-5-68. A catheter that is too short and only extends slightly into the vein is prone to dislodgement.

Fig-5-69. The short catheter is dislodged from the vein, resulting in paravenous infusion.

Solution: Using a longer catheter approximately 2 cm into the vein cm into the vein can prevent this. The additional length helps secure the catheter's position within the vein, reducing the risk of slipping out of the vein.

Inadequate depth of the needle-catheter system in the vein

Placing the needle-catheter sufficiently deep within the vein is a critical aspect of successful IV cannulation. This concept is vital because inadequate depth can lead to complications such as infiltration, where IV fluids enter the surrounding tissue instead of the vein, or extravasation, which can cause tissue damage with certain medications. Understanding and applying the appropriate depth ensures the catheter is properly positioned within the vein, securing effective medication delivery and minimizing patient discomfort.

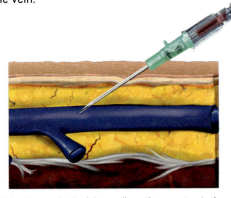

Fig-5-70. Inadequate depth of the needle-catheter system in the vein.

Common mistake: Avoid immediately threading the catheter upon observing a blood flashback. While a flashback indicates the needle is inserted into the vein, it doesn't confirm that the catheter is positioned within the vein. Advance the needle-catheter system slightly further into the lumen of the vein before attempting to slide the catheter in. Starting to thread the catheter before the needle and the catheter are fully in the lumen of the vein may lead to the catheter being lodged in the subcutaneous tissue instead of the vein, which is one of the most frequent errors.

Solution: A blood flashback is a sign that the needle tip is inside the vein lumen. Decrease the needle's angle and advance the needle-catheter system deeper in the vein.

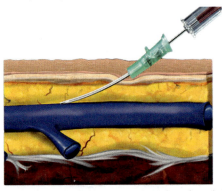

Fig-5-71. Premature threading might lead to the catheter being lodged in the subcutaneous tissue instead of the vein.

Too steep angle of needle insertion

Mistake: Failure to advance the needle at a low angle often results in the needle passing through the vein completely and a catheter placement into the subcutaneous tissue underneath the vein.

Fig-5-72. The angle of the needle-catheter insertion is too steep.

Fig-5-73. The catheter is placed into the subcutaneous tissue underneath the vein as the high angle will prevent the needle-catheter from advancing into the vein.

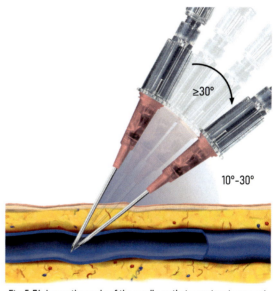

Solution: Lower the starting angle of the needle-catheter system to redirect the needle and advance the needle-catheter system sufficiently into the lumen of the vein.

Fig-5-74. Lower the angle of the needle-catheter system to prevent placing the catheter into the subcutaneous tissue.

Hematoma formation after catheter removal following an unsuccessful attempt

Hematoma formation following the removal of a catheter after an unsuccessful cannulation attempt is a common complication that underscores the importance of the strategy, precision and care during IV procedures. This issue often arises from the puncture of the vein wall, leading to blood leakage into the surrounding connective tissue.

Mistake: Failing an IV usually does not result in hematoma formation. However, a hematoma occurs quickly if the catheter is removed while leaving the tourniquet in place. Therefore, do not remove the catheter immediately after an unsuccessful cannulation attempt. Removing the needle-catheter will result in hematoma formation, necessitating the release of the tourniquet and extra time to stop the bleeding. This may complicate subsequent IV cannulation efforts.

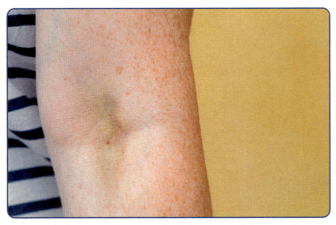
Fig-5-75. Hematoma formation after catheter removal. Removing the catheter eliminates the vein "plug".

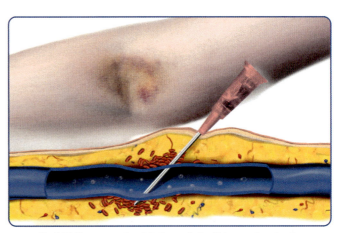
Fig-5-76. Hematoma after failed cannulation: Extravasation of red blood cells. The needle is seen piercing the posterior vein wall.

Solution: In case of a failed attempt, temporarily leave the catheter in place, allowing it to function as a venous plug within the vein. This will prevent bleeding and provide an opportunity to try again.

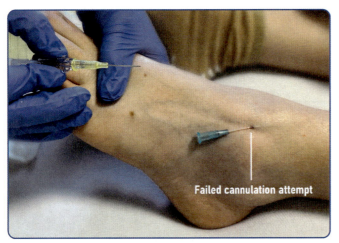
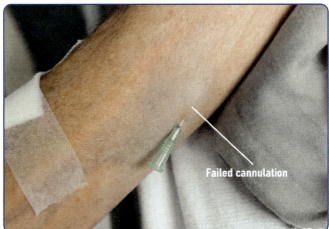
Fig-5-77. Leave the catheter in position in case of a failed attempt, allowing the catheter to function as a venous plug.

Starting too proximally on the vein

Mistake: Initiating an IV line too proximally on the vein can reduce alternative options for venous access if the first attempt is unsuccessful. A prior attempt may cause injury to the vein, increasing the risk of fluid leakage into the surrounding tissue when a second attempt is made distally to the initial insertion site.

Solution: Whenever possible, approach the vein distally, ensuring options for additional attempts proximally if the initial IV insertion attempt is unsuccessful.

> Access the videos for this section by scanning the QR code at the beginning of the chapter.

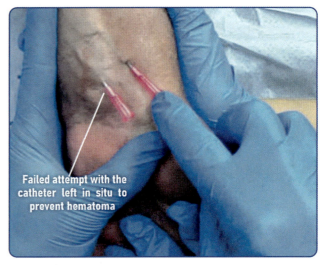
Fig-5-78. Approaching the vein distally allows for additional proximal attempts if the initial IV insertion attempt was unsuccessful.

Failure to secure catheter after insertion

Mistake: If the inserted catheter is left unsecured, it will likely become dislodged. This will lead to bleeding and hematoma formation, the need to compress the insertion site to stop the oozing, potential vein damage, and patient discomfort.

Solution: Secure the catheter immediately after insertion. Use tape or a specialized IV securing device to prevent accidental dislodgement. Prepare these securing materials beforehand so they are immediately available rather than having to gather them in the moments following insertion.

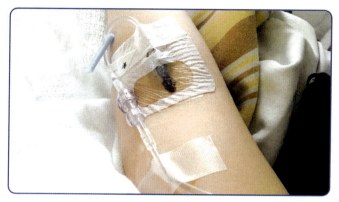

Fig-5-79. Secured IV catheter with an occlusive dressing and tape. This dressing allows easy inspection of the insertion site.

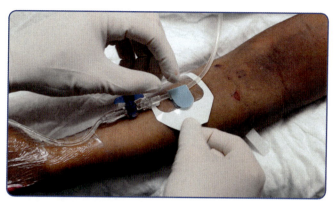

Fig-5-80. Specialized securing devices may be used to secure the IV tubing to prevent dislodgement. Shown here is a velcro securing system.

5.2 Cannulating complex veins

Difficult or invisible superficial veins

Navigating the challenge of difficult or invisible superficial veins is a critical skill for IV cannulation. This chapter discusses the complexities of identifying and accessing veins that are not readily visible or palpable, a common obstacle in patients with varying anatomical and physiological characteristics. Age, hydration status, and certain medical conditions can render veins less apparent, complicating IV procedures.

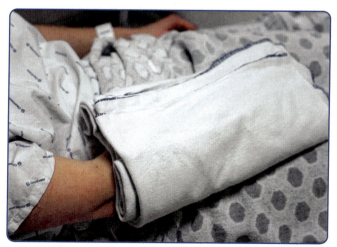

Fig-5-81. The application of warm towels or compresses helps to vasodilate the veins in patients with cold hands. Note that the semi-sitting position helps the gravity to fill the veins.

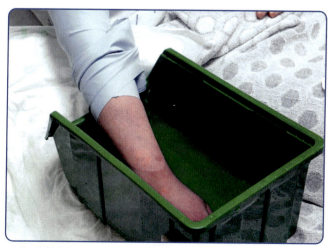

Fig-5-82. Soaking the patient's hand in warm water helps with vasodilation and increases the size of the veins.

05 Common mistakes and troubleshooting

Here are some tips to increase the likelihood of successful outcomes.

- **Hydration:** Adequate hydration can enhance venous volume. If possible, let the patient drink water, or sports drinks.
- **Heat application:** A warm compress, heating or warm towels cause vasodilation, increasing the size and visibility of the veins. Similarly, submersing the extremity in a warm bath can be useful to identify veins.
- **Patient position:** Where applicable, have the patient perform an exercise that activates the muscle pump and helps fill the vein with more blood. For example, if starting an IV at the wrist, have the patient clench and unclench their fist to increase vein prominence.
- **Tapping on skin:** Lightly tap the skin to induce mild venous vasodilation, increasing vein visibility.
- **Stabilize the vein:** Pull and stretch the skin distally to stabilize the vein during puncture. However, be careful not to apply too much pressure on the skin over the vein, as this can have the opposite effect and empty the vein, making the vein more difficult to cannulate.

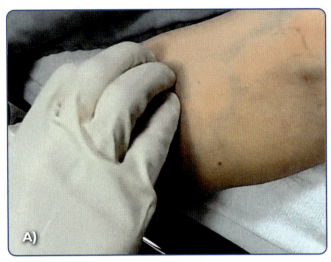 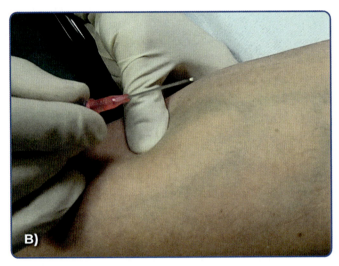

Fig-5-83. A) Lightly tap the skin to induce mild venous vasodilation, increasing vein visibility. B) Stabilize the vein during venipuncture using digital traction. Here, the left thumb is used to pull the skin and stabilize the vein to prevent rolling.

- **Bend the needle:** Consider bending the needle. While counterintuitive at first and requiring some practice, this tip can make all the difference in tight places where it is difficult to assume a low needle angle to sufficiently advance the needle-catheter system into the vein. Bending the needle-catheter system allows the elevation of the needle tip and ensures it stays within the superficial path of the vein. **Tip:** Needle bending is one of the pro's secrets.
- **Simulator training:** Consider practicing on a vein simulator and practice the needle bending in simulation first, before using this technique in patients.

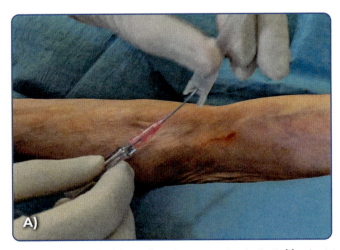 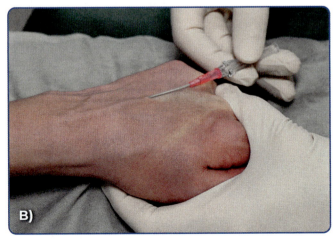

Fig-5-84. Bend the needle-catheter system to raise the tip (A) and maintain a low angle to ensure that the needle-catheter system remains within the superficial path of the vein (B).

- **Ultrasound guidance:** Using ultrasound is a no-brainer! Where the ultrasound machine, skill, and suitable deep veins are available, ultrasound can make all the difference. However, ultrasound is not efficient for superficial veins, as these lack sufficient depth to track the needle into the vein. Moreover, even the slightest pressure on the ultrasound transducer will flatten the superficial vein, making it impossible to cannulate.

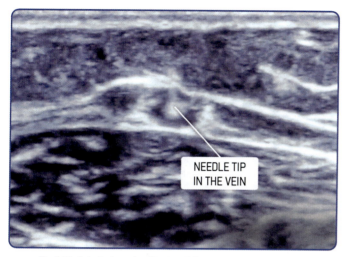

Fig-5-86. Out-of-plane visualization of the needle tip inside the vein. Fig-5-85. Use ultrasound guidance to visualize difficult veins.

- **Vein visualization technology:** Devices such as near-infrared vein finders highlight veins that are not visible to our eye. These devices use infrared or a bright light source to highlight the veins and are explained in more detail in *Chapter 11: Intravenous access training and assistance tools.*
- **Esmarch technique:** Wrap a rubber band (Esmarch, 10-15 cm or 4-6 inches in width) around the limb to encourage blood flow to the superficial veins to visualize them.
  - **Cannulation of the forearm:** Start at the axilla and extend the band to just below the elbow.
  - **Cannulation of the foot:** Wrap the band from the knee downward, covering the popliteal area.

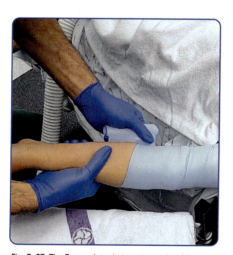 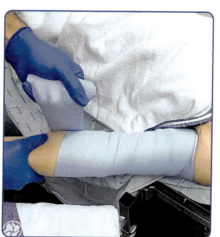 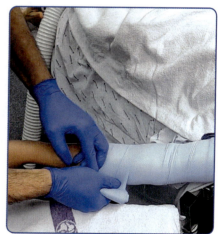

Fig-5-87. The Esmarch technique is used to fill the superficial veins with blood. Mechanism: Tourniquet effect and displacement shift of deep venous blood into superficial veins by elastic bandage application.

> **TIP**
> Watch the video to fully understand how to apply this very useful technique.

> Access the videos for this section by scanning the QR code at the beginning of the chapter.

Deep veins

Inserting a peripheral IV catheter into a deep vein is generally a more complex procedure than inserting one into a superficial vein, and it is typically not the first choice for peripheral IV access without ultrasound guidance. Deep veins are located further beneath the skin's surface, are typically larger, and are held firmly by surrounding connective tissue, preventing them from shifting or rolling. Although difficult to visualize, deeper veins are stronger and more stable than superficial veins. Rely on palpation to locate them.

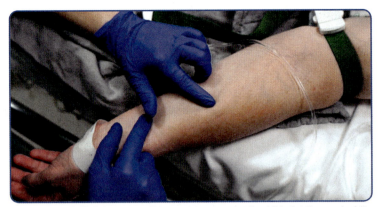

Fig-5-88. Palpate veins. Veins sometimes may not be visible, but they can be felt by their firmer feel compared to adjacent tissue.

Here are some practical tips.

- **Palpate:** Identify deep veins more by touch than by sight. Vein sometimes may not be visible, but they can be felt by their firmer feel compared to adjacent tissue.
- **Ultrasound:** Often necessary for deep vein cannulation to help locate the vein and to guide and confirm the needle's insertion. For step-by-step instructions on using ultrasound guidance for deep vein cannulation, we refer to *Chapter 9: Ultrasound-guided peripheral venous access*.
- **Use longer catheters:** A longer IV catheter is usually required to ensure the catheter can reach and remain within the deep vein. Depending on the planned therapy, the needle gauge may also need to be larger.
- **Optimize tourniquet position:** Position the tourniquet further up the arm to enhance venous distension, making even deeper veins more palpable.
- **Strategic limb positioning:** Adjust the limb's position to take advantage of gravity, which will help fill the veins, including the deeper veins.
- **Insertion angle:** The technique for deep vein cannulation requires a steeper insertion angle than for superficial in order to reach the veins.
- **Experience and training:** Because of the complexity and potential for complications (like deep tissue injury or nerve damage), this procedure is typically performed by a healthcare provider with advanced training and experience in deep vein cannulation.
- **Consider alternative access:** If locating a deep peripheral vein proves challenging, consider ultrasound-guided IV access of deeper veins or a CVC where long-term or high-volume access is necessary.

> **TIPS**
>
> - **Be mindful of risks:** Accessing deeper veins involves additional risks, such as potential harm to arteries, nerves, or surrounding structures.
> - **Approach with patience:** Unfortunately, multiple attempts are often part of the process. Apply an organized approach to multiple attempts to avoid repeating needle insertion in the same direction as previously failed attempts.
> - **Approach with care:** If unsuccessful after several attempts, do not hesitate to ask a colleague for assistance or take over.
> - **Troubleshooting:** Use an organized approach to multiple attempts. Change *ONLY ONE* element of the technique at a time. This prevents you from repeating the same error over and over again. "Fan" the needle angle left-to-right first while keeping the angle of the insertion constant. If unsuccessful, change the angle and repeat the "fan" technique. If done properly, this allows you to perform several meaningful attempts with different needle paths.

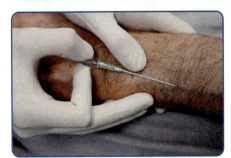 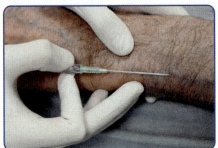 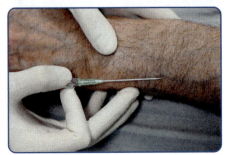

Fig-5-89. Fan-technique inserting the needle with small, organized changes in needle orientation to increase the success rate of cannulating a vein. This technique is particularly useful with deeper veins that can not be easily seen.

Tortuous or twisted veins

Tortuous veins are veins that have become enlarged and twisted, winding, or convoluted. Instead of following a relatively straight path, these veins have multiple curves or loops due to aging, atherosclerosis, hypertension, loss of connective tissue support, genetic defects, or diabetes mellitus.

Tortuous veins can present a challenge during IV cannulation or venipuncture, leading to multiple unsuccessful venous access attempts, increased patient discomfort, and a higher likelihood of complications such as bruising or hematoma.

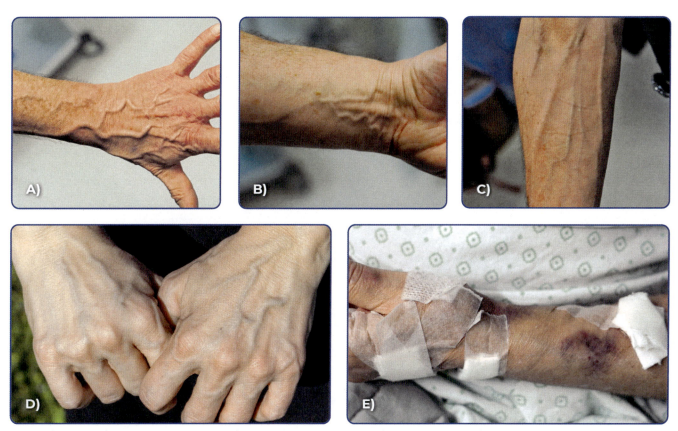

Fig-5-90. A) Tortuous veins on the dorsal side of the hand, B) on the palmar side of the hand, and C) in the upper extremity. D) Tortuous or twisted veins in the hand. E) Multiple unsuccessful venous access attempts due to tortuous veins.

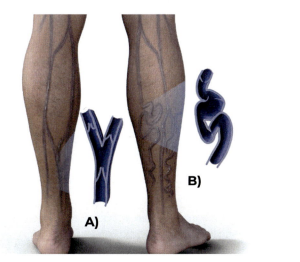
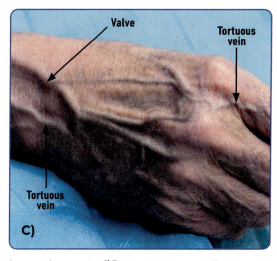

Fig-5-91. Examples of tortuous veins. A) Normal lesser saphenous vein. B) Tortuous, varicous lesser saphenous veins. C) Tortuous veins, prone to rolling.

05 Common mistakes and troubleshooting

Understanding tortuous veins

Though these veins are visible and easily palpable, and deceivingly simple to cannulate, they have lost their elasticity, making them prone to rolling when approached by the needle.

Strategies for tortuous veins

If a tortuous vein is the only option for IV cannulation, select one with visible branches (tributaries) that stabilize the needle entry or a relatively straight one.

- **Needle insertion:**
  - Maintain a low angle with the needle to minimize the risk of vein rolling.
  - Employ a swift-entry method; rapidly push the needle in to prevent the vein from rolling away. This technique is called the **"snake bite"** technique.
- **Counter traction method:**
  - Place a finger below the intended insertion site and gently pull the skin downward to create tension to stabilize the vein.

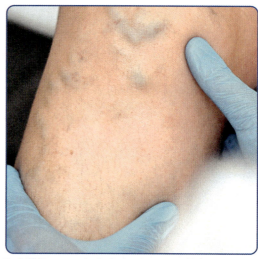

Fig-5-92. Tortuous veins in the lower extremity. Technique for vein stabilization.

Common mistake: Some advise stretching the skin on either side of the vein to create tension. This can be sometimes useful, however, this may cause the vein to appear less full and become harder to visualize. Additionally, it reduces the chances of blood return upon needle insertion.

Blown veins

Blown veins occur when the needle either goes through the vein or causes it to burst, resulting in blood leaking into nearby tissue. A bruise over the vein is often noticeable, sometimes with a mark from a previous attempt. This can happen due to using the wrong needle size, inserting a needle at the wrong angle into a vein that rolls easily, or fragile vein walls, common in older or chronically ill patients.

If an catheter insertion is attempted below a damaged vein, the infusion might go into the paravenous tissue instead of the bloodstream, causing problems (tissue inflammation, swelling) discomfort for the patient. Quickly and effectively dealing with a blown vein is important to avoid further problems, such as blood clot formation, infection, or delays in important IV treatment.

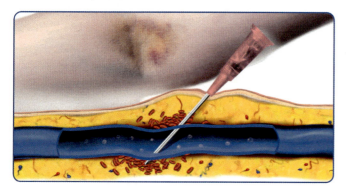

Fig-5-93. Blown vein resulting in hematoma formation.

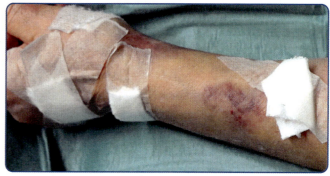

Fig-5-94. Multiple failed attempts in a patient will lead to bruising and discoloration due to the extravasation of hemoglobin.

What to do when a vein blows

- **Look proximally:** Attempt to insert the IV proximally to the blown vein. This is because the section of the vein above the injury remains intact and can still provide a reliable route for IV access. Inserting a catheter distally to the blown vein may result in paravenous leakage from the blown vein proximally.
- **Seek alternatives:** Choose a different vein or a different extremity all together.

Practical advice

- **Start distally:** Start at the most distal section of the vein when possible if there is no hematoma yet. This strategy may preserve more sections of the vein for use in subsequent attempts when IV cannulation proves difficult.
- **Catheter replacement:** A working catheter is usually replaced after 3-4 days of use. When inserting a new IV in the same vein, position it proximal from the previous insertion site or, if required, opt for an entirely different vein.

5.3 Troubleshooting failed cannulation

When vein cannulation fails it can be frustrating both patients and healthcare providers. Evaluate the cause of the failure. Reassess the chosen vein and consider selecting an alternative site if necessary. Below are some other tips clinicians should consider in case of a failed vein cannulation.

Check needle position

- **Problem:** If the needle fails to enter the vein, it might be positioned next to or below it, meaning that the needle-catheter system has not been inserted sufficiently deep into the vein. As a result, the catheter is 'pushed' against the vein wall, instead of into the lumen.
- **Intervention:**
  - Increase the counter traction on the skin.
  - Adjust the needle angle.
  - Change the insertion site or position of the patient's arm.

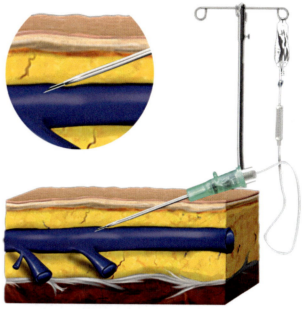

Fig-5-95. The needle is not inserted deep enough and the plastic cannula is positioned in the subcutaneous tissue.

Check for vein occlusion

- **Problem:** Difficulty inserting the needle into the vein might indicate a a clotted vein. A tell-tale sign is that the vein entry by the needle is difficult and the vein tends to roll instead of allowing the needle entering into the lumen.
- **Intervention**: Use ultrasound to inspect the vein. An occluded vein will resist collapsing when pressure is applied using the ultrasound transducer.

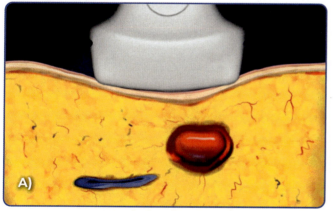 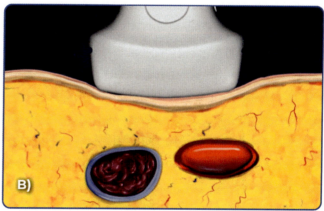

Fig-5-96. A) A healthy vein collapses when pressure is applied using the ultrasound transducer. B) An occluded, thrombosed vein will resist collapsing.

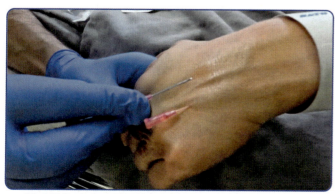

Fig-5-97. Retain the failed catheter as a venous plug to mitigate bleeding.

Start over with vein cannulation

- **Problem:** Immediate removal of a failed cannula can lead to profuse bleeding.
- **Intervention:** It is often best to initiate a new attempt at a new insertion site with a new needle while retaining the failed catheter as a venous plug to mitigate bleeding.

> Access the videos for this section by scanning the QR code at the beginning of the chapter.

05 Common mistakes and troubleshooting

Consider leaving the tourniquet on

- **Problem:** The removal of the tourniquet immediately after a failed attempt will undo the effort it took to distend the patient's peripheral veins.
- **Solution:** Leave the failed catheter without the needle in sight and consider keeping the tourniquet in place for another attempt. This can minimize the risk of bleeding and hematoma and save time until the next attempt is successful. Remove the failed catheter after IV access is suffessfully established.

5.4 Avoid vein cannulation at valves

When attempting IV insertion, avoid areas at or immediately below a venous valve, as they can complicate the insertion procedure for the following reasons:

- **Difficult insertion:** Valves can obstruct the passage of the cannula, making insertion more difficult.
- **Risk of damage:** Damaging a valve can lead to complications such as thrombophlebitis.
- **Inefficient flow:** If a catheter tip is positioned near or against a valve, it can impede the flow of fluids or medications.
- **Increased risk of occlusion:** Catheters placed near valves have a higher tendency to become occluded.
- **Patient discomfort:** Cannulating a vein at a valve can be uncomfortable to the patient.
- **Potential for infiltration:** If the catheter is not positioned correctly due to a valve, there is a risk of paravenous infusion into the surrounding tissues, causing swelling and pain.
- **Reduced catheter longevity:** Catheters placed near valves may not last as long and require more frequent replacement, leading to more discomfort for the patient and additional procedures.
- **Blood draw can be difficult:** The valve may obstruct the catheter, and there is a high risk of vein rupture if the valve gets punctured during insertion.

For these reasons, when performing venipuncture, palpate the vein carefully and choose a site that feels smooth and free of the palpable "bumps" or resistance that might indicate the presence of a valve. Identifying and avoiding valves can increase the chances of successful IV cannulation, reduce patient discomfort, and decrease the potential for complications.

Here's how to identify valves:

Palpation

- Use your fingers to palpate the vein gently.
- Valves typically feel like slight "bumps" or "knots" alongside the course of the vein.
- If a noticeable "bump" followed by a depression or void is felt while palpating a vein segment, this may indicate the presence of a valve.

Tourniquet application

- Apply a tourniquet above the site being assessed.
- This causes veins to distend, making it easier to palpate and identify any irregularities or bumps, which could indicate valves.

Visual inspection

- Valves can sometimes cause a visible bifurcation or branching in the vein.
- Look for areas where the vein appears to split or has a noticeable widening.

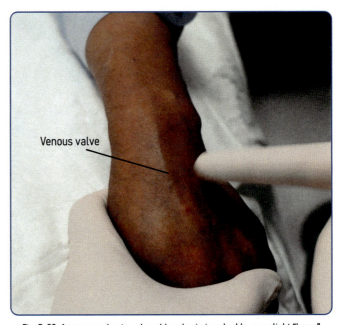

Fig-5-98. A venous valve in a dorsal hand vein is palpable as a slight "bump" or "knot" within the vein.

Transillumination

- Use a transilluminator or "vein light" to illuminate the subcutaneous structures *(Chapter 11: Intravenous access training and assistance tools)*.
- This can highlight the path of the vein and show areas with potential valves.

Ultrasound

- An increasingly commonly used method for diffucult IV placement.
- Ultrasound can visualize the vein's anatomy, including valves, bifurcations, and diameter.
- It can show real-time blood flow, with valves appearing as echogenic (bright) structures interrupting the vein's lumen.

Assess blood flow

- Press distal to the site being assessed and release. If the blood flow stops momentarily and resumes, it might indicate proximity to a valve.
- **Note:** This method is not foolproof but can provide an additional clue.

Experience and training

- As with many clinical skills, the ability to identify veins and their valves improves with experience and training. Over time, practitioners become more adept at distinguishing the feel of a valve from other structures or irregularities in the vein.

5.5 What to do when the catheter cannot be advanced

If resistance is encountered and the catheter cannot advance despite obtaining a flashback of blood, do not force it, as the needle tip may be stuck against a valve or the vein's wall.

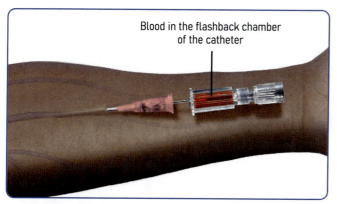 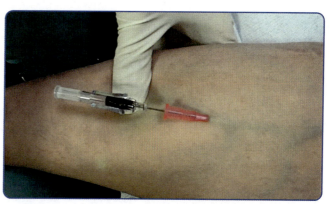

Fig-5-99. Obtaining a flashback of blood does not necessarily mean the catheter can advance as the needle tip may be stuck against a valve or the vein's wall.

Here are the steps to consider:

- **Retraction and repositioning:** Carefully retract the needle slightly before gently trying to advance the catheter again. This minor adjustment helps to reposition the needle within the vein, allowing the catheter to move forward smoothly. If it appears that the catheter-needle assembly is not inserted deep enough, consider advancing the assembly sightly deeper at a low angle into the lumen of the vein. Only then attempt to thread the catheter over the needle.
- **Adjust the insertion angle:** Use the correct insertion angle. Upon obtaining a flashback, lower the angle of the needle-catheter system to be almost parallel to the skin before advancing further. This adjustment aligns the catheter with the vein, facilitating smoother entry.
- **Consider using the "Floating technique"** when you suspect that the catheter may be stopped by a valve:
  1. Start by inserting the needle just deep enough to secure the catheter's tip within the vein.
  2. Pull back the needle slightly, exposing part of the catheter.
  3. Slowly flush while cautiously advancing the catheter.
  4. Continue flushing and advancing until the catheter is entirely inside the vein.
     - Flushing the catheter helps to open valves, fills and widens the vein, and reduces the risk of puncturing through the other side of the vein.

5.6 IV fluid does not flow

When the IV fluid refuses to flow, several factors might be responsible. Understanding the cause is essential for effective troubleshooting. Below are the common causes with their respective solution. Troubleshoot this situation in this order.

- **Kinked catheter (common):** Inspect the catheter to rule out a kink. Try to unkink the catheter, keeping in mind that this often requires catheter replacement.
- **Clotted catheter (common):** Use a small syringe filled with saline to "flush" the catheter and re-establish the flow. Using a small syringe allows for generating higher injection pressure needed for catheter flushing (e.g., 3 mL) when the catheter is obstructed. When successful, a small, fresh thrombus dissolves in the bloodstream or is caught in the lung circulation without consequences.
- **Kinked or twisted IV tubing:** Straighten the IV tubing and verify it is free from obstructions or bends.
- **Catheter position:** Alter the position of the patient's limb or adjust their overall position. Even minor repositioning can help re-establish the flow.
- **Catheter against the vein wall:** Gently aspirate and flush with saline to reposition the catheter tip. If unsuccessful, consider insertion at a new site.

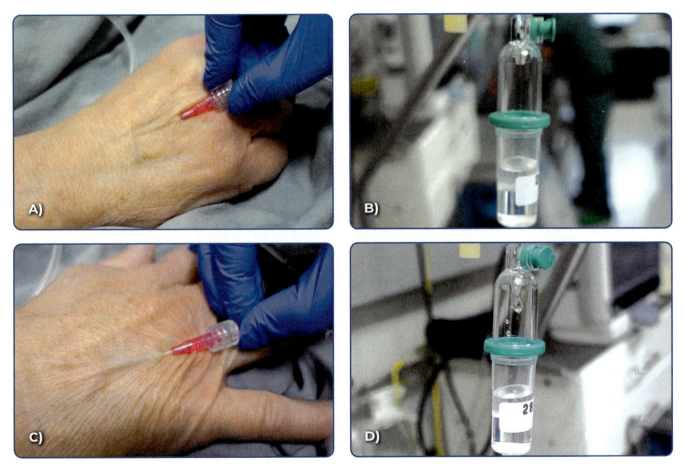

Fig-5-100. Examples of common causes of the absence of IV flow. A) The catheter is positioned against the vein wall. B) The IV fluid refuses to flow. C) Pull back the catheter gently to adjust its position. D) The IV fluid will flow again.

- **Infiltration (fluid in surrounding tissue):** Stop the infusion and remove the IV catheter. Choose a new cannulation site and reinsert. Elevate the affected limb and apply a cold or warm compress, depending on the type of infiltrated fluid.
- **Blocked filter or valve:** Check all parts of the IV system, including any filters or valves, and replace them if needed.
- **IV bag position:** Hang the IV bag above the insertion site to promote flow aided by gravity.
- **Empty IV bag:** Replace the IV bag.
- **Air in IV line:** Remove air from the tubing by priming the line.

5.7 Large vein cannulation with a large-bore IV catheter

The expertise in inserting large-bore IV catheters during acute scenarios is essential for doctors, paramedics, and nurses taking care of critically ill or injured patients. Large-bore IV lines are frequently needed in the emergency department, trauma victims, or in the OR when major blood loss is anticipated. Most medical professionals become proficient at establishing small-gauge IV lines over time. However, inserting large-bore catheters, especially in patients requiring substantial IV fluids or blood for resuscitation, presents a greater challenge. One might assume that cannulating these prominent, large veins would be straightforward. However, they can be challenging and require skill and expertise.

Characteristics of large veins

- **Elasticity:** Larger veins may exhibit wall elasticity, which may cause them to "roll" or shift away from the needle during puncture attempts.
- **Wall thickness:** The walls of larger veins are thicker, requiring more force to penetrate, increasing the risk of rolling or going through the posterior wall of the vein.
- **Surrounding tissue:** There might be more surrounding adipose tissue or muscle around larger veins, making them harder to visualize and access.
- **The angle of approach:** The optimal angle for cannulating larger veins may differ from that of smaller veins, requiring adjustments in technique.
- **Risk of complications:** A failed attempt at cannulating a large vein carries a larger risk of complications such as hematoma formation, further complicating subsequent attempts.
- **Catheter length:** The typically longer length of large-bore catheters makes the insertion technique and handling more challenging.

Successful cannulation, especially in challenging or emergency scenarios, requires a combination of knowledge, skill, and the appropriate technique. Here are some general strategies and techniques that can be employed to enhance success rates in cannulating large veins with large-bore IV catheters.

- **Traction technique:** Applying gentle downward traction on the skin distal to the insertion site can help stabilize rolling veins and make them tenser and easier to puncture. However, be careful here; use firm yet gentle traction to prevent compression of the vein's volume, making it much more difficult to cannulate.

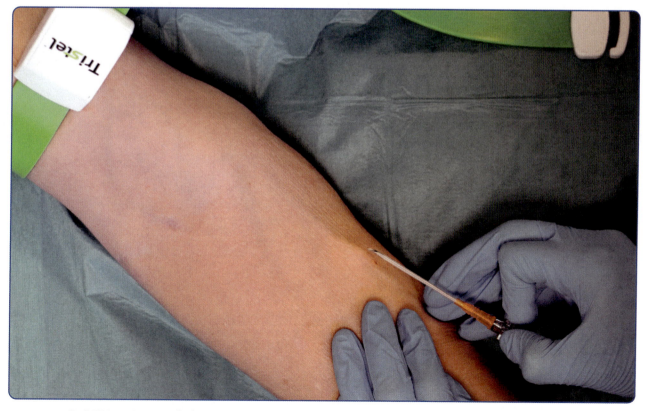

Fig-5-101. Large IV catheter (14G), insertion and technique of stabilizing the skin by digital traction before needle-catheter insertion.

- **Bevel-up needle:** Starting with the bevel facing up will facilitate the ease of vein entry and decrease the risk of skimming over the vein. Bevel-up also helps the blood enter the needle quicker and appear in the flashback chamber. *Rationale:* A bevel-down approach may obstruct the bevel with the vein's intima, causing delayed flushing or unnoticed needle passage through the vein.
- **Seldinger technique:** For difficult cannulations, the modified Seldinger technique, involving guidewire insertion followed by the catheter, can be useful.

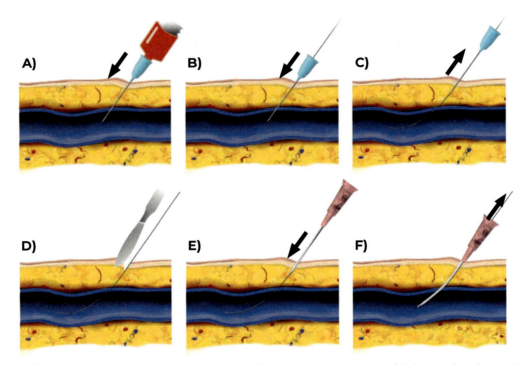

Fig-5-102. The Seldinger technique, involving guidewire insertion followed by the catheter, can be useful when cannulating larger veins. A) Needle insertion into the vein. B) Guidewire insertion. C) Needle removal. D) Using a skin dilator or scalpel "nick" (optional). E) The catheter is slid over the guidewire. F) The guidewire is removed.

- **Appropriate angle of entry:** Traditional books on IV cannulations often advocate beginning with a steeper angle to penetrate the skin, then flattening the angle as the vein is approached. However, we advise against this approach. Using a steep angle to enter the vein may pose challenges in adjusting the needle without unintentionally removing it or going through the vein's posterior (opposite) wall. This quickly leads to hematoma formation, especially in larger veins. Therefore, we advise starting with a low angle to reduce the risk of going through the posterior wall.

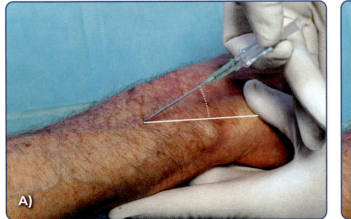
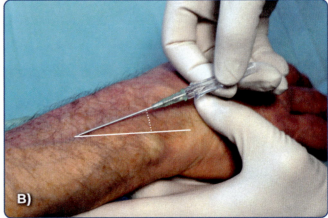

Fig-5-103. A) Using a steep angle to enter the vein may pose challenges in adjusting the needle without unintentionally removing it or going through the vein's posterior wall. B) Start with a low angle to reduce the risk of going through the posterior wall.

- **Stabilize the vein:** Using the non-dominant hand to stabilize the vein reduces the likelihood of the vein rolling away. Remember to avoid maneuvers that cause pressure over the vein, which can squeeze the blood out and make it more difficult to cannulate.
- **Apply short and controlled fast-forward movements:** When encountering resistance while attempting to cannulate the vein, it is imperative to use short, fast, yet controlled forward movements. This approach, we refer to as the "snake bite" technique, helps needle entry through the thick-walled or calcified veins, as opposed to pushing the vein away with a slow approach. Remember that the tips of large bore needle-catheter systems, such as 14G, 16G, or 18G, are not as sharp as the smaller gauge needle tips. As such, they may push the thick-walled veins away from the needle instead of penetrating them. Practicing the snake bite technique is essential for successfully penetrating the vein wall. However, it's important to ensure these movements are short and controlled to prevent accidental puncture of the vein's posterior wall.

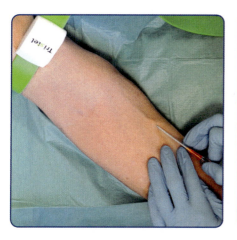
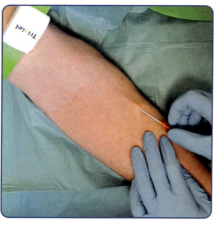
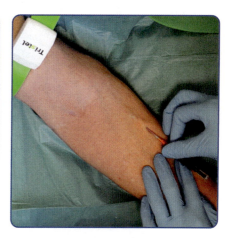

Fig-5-104. When inserting a large IV catheter (e.g., 14G) it is imperative to use fast, short yet controlled forward movements. This will help needle entry through the thick-walled or calcified veins.

- **Stay calm and take time:** There's a natural inclination to rush, especially in emergencies. However, staying calm and methodical leads to better outcomes at venous cannulation.
- **Ultrasound guidance:** Ultrasound guidance allows for real-time visualization of the vein, adjacent structures, and the needle trajectory. Ultrasound can increase the success rate and decrease complications. However, in urgent situations, like trauma cases, immediate large-bore catheter insertion is often paramount, without the luxury of the additional time required for setting up an ultrasound.

By understanding the inherent challenges of inserting large-bore IV catheters in larger veins and employing these strategies, you can increase the success rates and reduce potential complications.

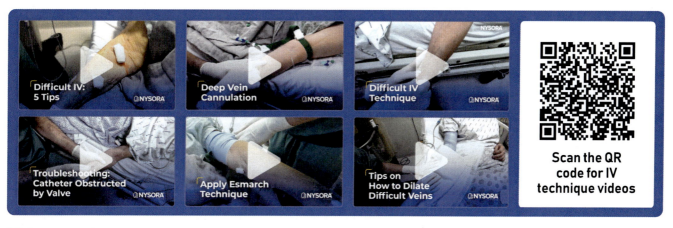

05 Common mistakes and troubleshooting

5.8 Algorithms

Troubleshooting

COMMON MISTAKES	SOLUTIONS
Wrong choice of the catheter - Catheter too short	Choose a longer catheter (1-2 cm)
The needle-catheter system is not deep enough inside the vein	Decrease the needle angle and advance the needle-catheter deeper in the vein
Too steep needle-catheter insertion angle	Lower the starting angle of the needle-catheter system
Hematoma formation after immediate catheter removal following a failed attempt	Leave the catheter in the vein as a venous plug
Starting too proximally on the vein	Approach the vein distally so that additional options remain possible
Failure to secure the catheter after insertion	Secure the catheter immediately after insertion

Troubleshooting

Difficult or invisible superficial veins	Deep veins	Tortuous or twisted veins	Blown veins
Hydration Heat application Patient positioning Tap on the skin Stabilize the vein Bend the needle Ultrasound guidance Vein finders Esmarch technique (rubber band to encourage blood flow)	Rely on touch Ultrasound guidance Use a longer catheter Optimize tourniquet position Limb position – use gravity Use a steeper insertion angle Consider alternative access: central venous catheter	Opt for a vein with branches or a relatively straight vein Maintain a low angle during insertion Contemplate bending the needle Use a swift-entry method Use the counter traction method Do NOT stretch the skin on either side of the vein	Insert the IV proximal to the blown vein Seek alternatives

Scan the QR code for IV technique videos

NAVIGATING FAILED NEEDLE INSERTION

Check needle position	• Increase the countertraction on the skin • Adjust the needle angle • Change the insertion site or position of the patient's arm
Check for vein occlusion	• Use ultrasound to examine the vein
Start over with vein cannulation	• Do NOT adjust the needle position under the skin • Start a new attempt at a new insertion site with a new needle • Keep the failed catheter as a venous plug
Leave the tourniquet on	• Leave the tourniquet on for further attempts to minimize bleeding

IDENTIFY AND AVOID VENOUS VALVES

- Palpate the vein. Valves feel like bumps or protrusions
- Apply an additional tourniquet to make it easier to palpate the veins
- Inspect the vein visually
- Use a transilluminator to illuminate subcutaneous structures
- Use ultrasound to identify valves and detect disruptions in blood flow by valves
- Assess blood flow by pressing the site and releasing: the blood flow stops and resumes near a valve

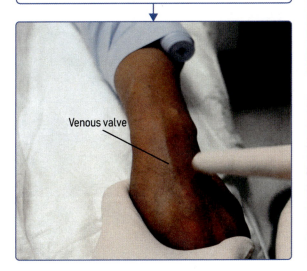

Venous valve

WHAT TO DO WHEN THE CATHETER CANNOT BE ADVANCED

- Do not force the catheter, as the needle tip may be stuck against a valve or vein wall
- Advance the needle-catheter deeper into the vein
- Lower the angle of the needle to be almost parallel to the skin
- Consider the 'floating technique' when the needle tip encounters a valve
    1. Start by inserting the needle just enough to secure the catheter's tip within the vein
    2. Pull back the needle slightly, leaving part of the catheter exposed
    3. Slowly flush while advancing the catheter
    4. Continue flushing and advancing until the catheter is entirely inside the vein

IV FLUID DOES NOT FLOW

Clotted catheter	Use a small syringe filled with saline to "flush" the catheter
Kinked catheter	Try to unkink the catheter or even replace the catheter
Catheter position	Alter the position of the patient's limb or their overall position
Catheter against the vein wall	Aspirate and flush the catheter with saline to reposition the catheter tip If unsuccessful, reinsert the IV at a new site
Infiltration of fluid in tissue	Remove the IV catheter Reinsert the IV at a new site Elevate the limb and apply a cold or warm compress as appropriate
Blocked filter or valve	Check all parts of the IV system and replace if needed
IV bag position	Hang the IV bag above the insertion site
Empty IV bag	Replace the IV bag
Air in IV line	Remove air from the tubing by priming the line or aspirating with a syringe.

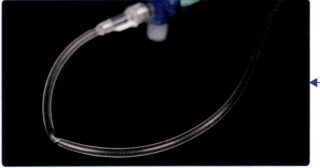

05 Common mistakes and troubleshooting

LARGE VEIN CANNULATION WITH A LARGE-BORE IV CATHETER

Challenges of large veins
- Increased vessel elasticity, causing veins to roll
- Increased wall thickness, requiring more force to penetrate
- Calcified venous wall
- Surrounded by adipose tissue or muscles, making them harder to visualize
- The optimal angle for cannulation deviates from smaller veins
- More risk of complications
- The longer length of large-bore catheters challenges the insertion technique

Strategies to enhance success rates
- Apply gentle downward traction on the skin distal to the insertion site
- Insert the needle with the bevel up
- Use the modified Seldinger technique (guidewire insertion followed by the catheter)
- Start with a low angle from the start to penetrate the skin
- Use the non-dominant hand to stabilize the vein
    - Avoid maneuvers that cause pressure over the vein as this may squeeze the blood out of the vein, making its lumen smaller
- Apply short and controlled forward movements
    - The 14G, 16G, and 18G needle tips are not as sharp as smaller gauge needle tips and may need a faster insertion
    - These needles tend to push the thick-walled veins away, resulting in vein "rolling"
    - Consider using US

06

Scan the QR code for IV technique videos

IV CATHETERIZATION IN LESS COMMON ANATOMICAL SITES

When the typical locations for IV insertion become unavailable, an IV catheter may have to be inserted in an alternate location rather than the frequently used peripheral veins of the arms and legs. Here's what you need to know.

6.1 Cannulation of veins in the foot

While less common, establishing IV access in the foot becomes indispensable in certain clinical scenarios. Patients with extensive burns or trauma or those who have had multiple previous venous access attempts may require cannulation at this alternative site. Furthermore, the foot is frequently chosen for vein cannulation in pediatric patients. Foot cannulation demands a thorough understanding of the foot's vascular anatomy, strict adherence to an aseptic technique, and careful consideration of patient comfort and mobility.

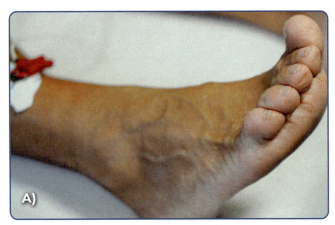
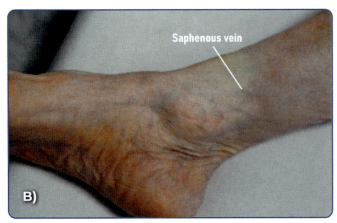

Fig-6-105. Examples of veins in the foot. A) Dorsum of foot venous network. B) Saphenous vein.

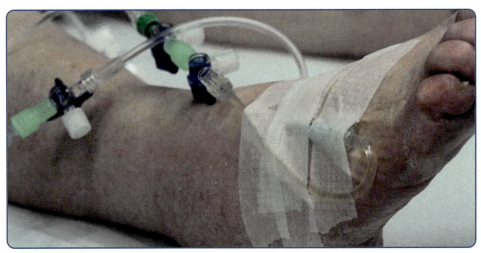

Fig-6-106. Secured peripheral IV catheter inserted in one of the veins belonging to the dorsal venous network.

Indications	Complications
• Alternative access • Pediatric patients • Patients with chronic illness such as chronic kidney disease where repeated venous access is needed and other sites are compromised • Long-term medication administration	• Infection • Phlebitis • Extravasation • Thrombophlebitis • Thrombosis • Hematoma • Peripheral edema • Impaired circulation • Movement restrictions • Pain as the foot is a sensitive area

When access in the upper extremities is not available, successful IV cannulation in the foot requires careful technique and consideration, especially since this area can be more sensitive, have thicker skin, tortuous veins, and be more challenging. Here are some tips for IV placement in the foot.

Patient position: Have the patient lie down and position the foot for easy access.
- Lowering the foot below the heart level aids to venous distension, making the veins more prominent and easier to access. This can be achieved by positioning the patient in a semi-sitting position.
- In some cases, particularly if lying down isn't possible, the patient can sit upright with the legs hanging off the edge of the bed. Gravity will help fill the peripheral veins in the lower extremity, aiding in vein visibility and accessibility.

Vein selection: Look for a suitable vein on the dorsum of the foot. These veins are often more superficial and easier to cannulate. Avoid veins over bony prominences (one exception: saphenous vein).

Warm compress: Applying a warm compress or towel to the foot for a few minutes can help dilate the veins, making cannulation easier. Consider using a forced-air device to warm up the patient/extremity (e.g., Bair Hugger™).

Hygiene and antiseptic: Clean the area thoroughly with an antiseptic solution to reduce the infection risk.

Tourniquet application: Apply a tourniquet above the ankle to engorge the veins. Ensure it's tight enough to restrict venous return without affecting arterial flow.

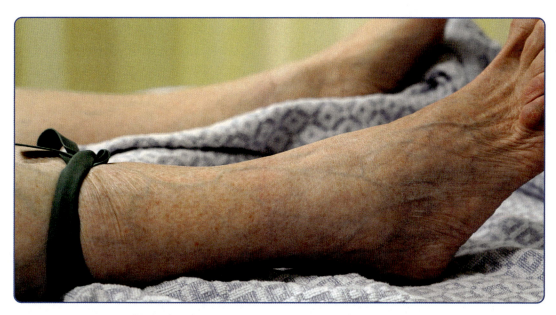

Fig-6-107. Apply a tourniquet above the ankle to engorge the veins of the foot.

Use a smaller gauge needle: Consider using a smaller needle gauge for foot cannulations, as foot veins can be smaller and more fragile.

Needle insertion: Gently insert the needle at a low angle (15 to 30 degrees) with the bevel up. Advance the needle slowly while looking for a blood flashback.

Stabilize the vein: The foot veins can be more mobile, so use your non-dominant hand to stabilize the vein during needle insertion.

Secure the cannula: Once the needle is in the vein, advance the cannula and remove the needle. Secure the cannula with tape, ensuring it doesn't obstruct the blood flow.

Check for proper flow: Connect to the IV line and confirm that fluids flow correctly without swelling or discomfort.

Comfort and protection: Place a protective dressing to secure the IV and ensure the patient is comfortable, as the foot can be a more sensitive area for an IV.

Monitoring: Regularly monitor the IV site for signs of infiltration, infection, or phlebitis.

Patient instructions: Instruct the patient to notify the staff if they feel any pain, burning, or discomfort at the IV site.

IV cannulation in the foot should be approached cautiously and is typically reserved for situations where other sites are not viable. Due to the potential complications, this technique should be performed by healthcare professionals who are more experienced in IV therapy.

Saphenous vein cannulation

Saphenous vein cannulation is a useful technique for securing venous access when traditional sites are inaccessible. This technique involves inserting a catheter into the saphenous vein at the inner ankle, which is particularly useful for administering fluids and medications. This is also vital for emergency vascular access in neonates, infants, and adults when conventional options are unsuitable.

For saphenous vein cannulation, especially in neonates and infants, sizes typically range from 24G to 22G, allowing for the safe administration of necessary treatments with minimal discomfort. When saphenous access is indicated in adults, slightly larger sizes (18G-20G) may be used, depending on the vein's diameter and the intended use; whether for fluid resuscitation, medication administration, or blood sampling.

Step-by-step technique of IV cannulation of the saphenous vein

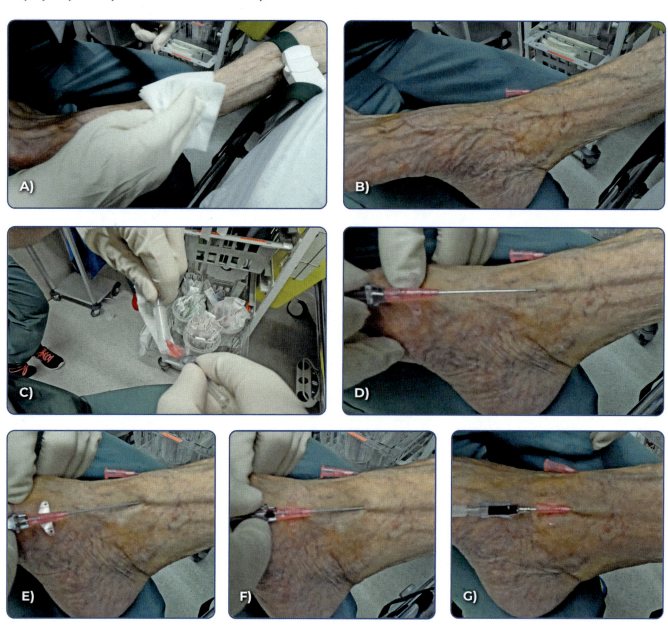

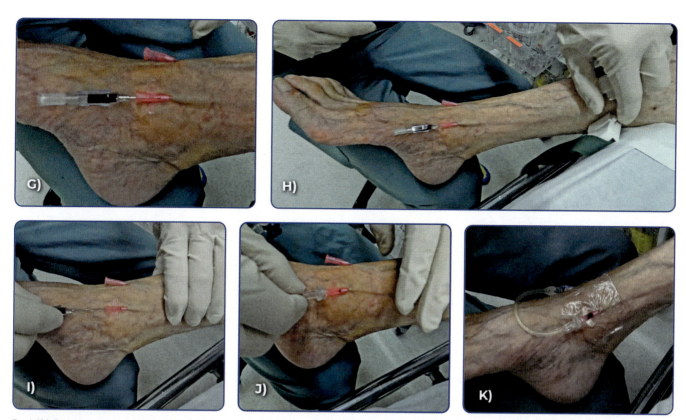

Fig-6-108. Saphenous vein cannulation. A) Disinfect the insertion site. B) Leave the failed catheter in the vein to function as a venous plug. C) Bend the needle to ease catheter insertion. D) Stabilize the foot to ease catheter insertion. E) Insert the needle at an angle of 15-30 degrees relative to the skin. F) Blood in the flashback chamber indicates that the needle is inside the vein. G) Advance the catheter an additional 1-2 mm to ensure that the catheter tip is also in the vein. H) Release the tourniquet. I) Retract the needle. J) Attach the IV tubing to the catheter. K) Secure the catheter with an occlusive dressing.

NOTE

These images show a successful saphenous vein cannulation in a patient with a previously failed attempt in the dorsum of the foot. Note that the IV catheter was left in situ at the unsuccessful attempt to prevent hematoma formation.

TIPS

- The foot's skin is often thicker, which can pose a greater challenge when attempting to puncture the vein.
- Proceed with confidence and a steady hand, as hesitation may cause the veins to shift or "roll".
- While larger veins seem tempting for those new to the procedure, they often demand greater expertise. Use smaller veins supported by tributaries to enhance stability and increase the likelihood of a successful insertion.
- During needle insertion, use your palm to extend the foot, thereby stretching the skin and veins, making them more stable and easier to visualize.

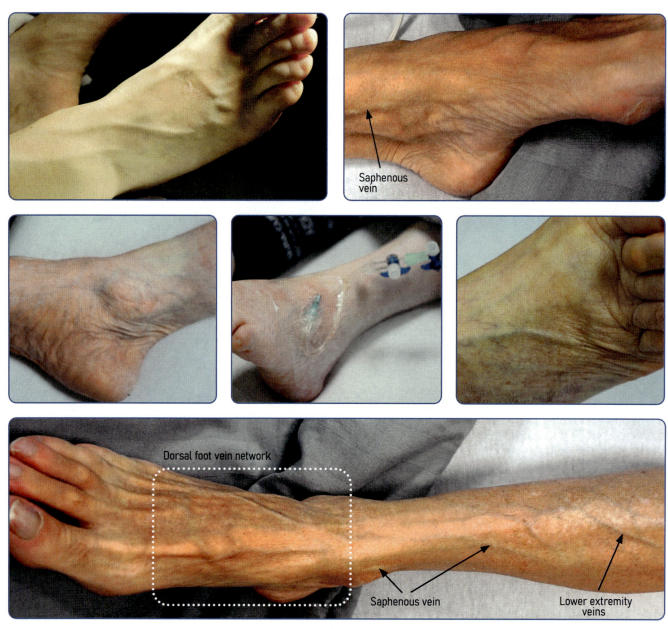

Fig-6-109. Examples of foot veins suitable for IV access.

6.2 Superficial veins over the chest, breast, and thigh area

The superficial veins in the chest, breast, and thigh area serve as alternative IV access points during urgent situations when standard access sites are impractical or unavailable. Cannulating superficial veins over the chest, breast, and shoulders can be a necessary alternative in patients where IV access in the hands and arms is difficult or impossible.

Chest area: The superficial veins in the chest area, including the cephalic vein running along the lateral aspect of the arm and potentially extending into the chest, offer potential sites for IV cannulation. Precision and a thorough understanding of chest anatomy are paramount to avoid vital structures.

Breast area: Cannulation in the breast area is generally avoided due to the high density of lymphatic vessels and nodes, as well as the potential for causing discomfort and psychological distress to patients. The infection risk and lymphedema make this area less desirable for IV placement. Therefore, this choice is reserved only for dire situations when no other access is available.

Thigh area: The superficial veins of the thigh, such as the great saphenous vein and its network at the medial aspect of the thigh, can be considered for IV cannulation in specific circumstances when other sites are not viable. The thigh area provides a large surface area, but cannulation here can be challenging due to the depth of veins and the increased risk of thrombophlebitis. Proper technique and patient positioning are important for success and to minimize discomfort.

In all these areas, the site choice for IV cannulation must be guided by the clinician's expertise, patient anatomy, and specific clinical situations. It's essential to weigh the benefits against potential risks and complications, ensuring informed consent is obtained from the patient or their guardian. Additionally, adherence to strict aseptic techniques and ongoing assessment of the cannulation site for signs of infection or infiltration are vital for patient safety and the therapy's success.

Indications	Complications
· Alternative access · Short-term IV access (bridging time until an IV is possible elsewhere) · Emergencies (resuscitation) · Anesthesia · Blood drawing	· Thrombosis · Infiltration · Extravasation · Phlebitis · Hematoma · Infection

Here are some tips for performing IV access using superficial chest, breast, or thigh areas.

Patient consent and comfort: Explain the procedure to the patient, obtain informed consent, and ensure the patient's comfort and privacy.

Vein selection: Carefully inspect and palpate the chest, breast, and thigh areas to identify suitable superficial veins. Look for straight, well-distended veins that have good blood flow.

Use a tourniquet, if appropriate: It may help distend the veins, but its application can be challenging in these areas. If used, ensure it's not too tight and remove it as soon as possible.

Maintain privacy and dignity: Use drapes or garments to expose only the necessary area for cannulation, maintaining the patient's dignity, especially when accessing more sensitive areas like the breast.

Infection control: Clean the chosen site thoroughly with an antiseptic solution, using a circular motion from the center outward.

Gentle technique: Use a gentle approach when inserting the needle, as veins in these areas can be more fragile and superficial. A smaller gauge needle may be more appropriate. Keep in mind the tortuous nature of these veins.

Secure the cannula: Use tape or an appropriate dressing, ensure it doesn't pressure the skin or underlying tissues.

Regular monitoring: Frequently monitor the IV site for signs of infiltration, infection, or discomfort, given the sensitivity of these areas.

Documentation: Record the procedure details including the cannulation site, the needle gauge, and any patient concerns or complications.

Educate the patient: Inform patients about signs of complications such as swelling, redness, pain, or heat at the IV site, and instruct them to report these immediately.

Alternative techniques: Consider other methods of vascular access if superficial veins are not suitable or if the patient experiences significant discomfort.

Cannulating veins in these areas requires a higher level of skill and should only be attempted by healthcare professionals experienced in IV therapy. Patient safety, comfort, and privacy should be the primary considerations throughout the procedure.

> Access the videos for this section by scanning the QR code at the beginning of the chapter.

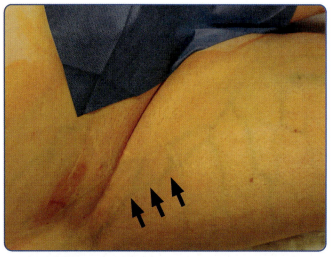

Fig-6-110. The proximal saphenous vein of the saphenous vein network is a viable alternative in patients with difficult venous access.

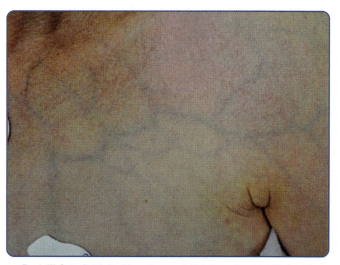

Fig-6-111. Superficial shoulder veins are viable alternatives in patients with difficult venous access in the upper or lower extremities.

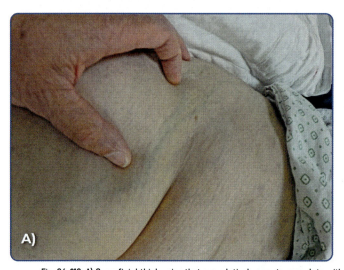
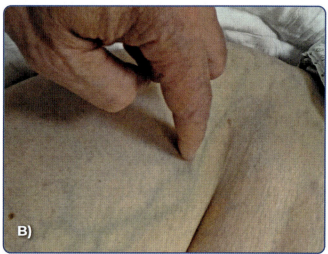

Fig-06-112. A) Superficial thigh veins that are relatively easy to cannulate with a small gauge IV catheter. B) These veins are easily visible, palpable, and straight, and there is no need to use a tourniquet.

TIPS

- Pay close attention to detect fluid infiltration since it is harder to notice in the chest, shoulder, and thigh areas.
- Aim to replace the IV promptly; catheterization at these sites is intended for short-term use only.

Scan the QR code for IV technique videos

6.3 Intraosseous cannulation

Intraosseous (IO) access is used to inject medications or fluids directly into the marrow cavity of a large bone, typically the proximal tibia, distal tibia, or humerus. The bone marrow acts as a non-collapsible vein that can absorb medication, fluids, or blood products, providing immediate access to the circulatory system. IO access is a life-saving procedure in emergency medicine, particularly when other forms of vascular access are not available or feasible. Avoid IO access in case of fractures, burns, cellulitis, or infection at the intended site and in patients with osteogenesis imperfecta.

Indications	Complications
- Repeated IV failures - Dehydration in vulnerable populations (pediatric or elderly patients) - Mass casualty scenarios to gain quick access - Pediatric resuscitation as the IO route is often faster and more reliable - Urgent administration of medication, fluids, or blood products	- Incomplete penetration of the needle into the medullary space - Pain - Compartment syndrome - Infection - Fluid extravasation - Epiphyseal plate necrosis - Fracture - Bent IO needle - Osteomyelitis

Here are some tips for effective IO cannulation.

Patient position: Place the patient supine.

Landmark identification

- **Adults**
    - **Proximal tibia:** The insertion point is 1-2 cm (0.3-0.8 inches) below and medial to the tibial tuberosity.
    - **Proximal humerus:** Rotate the humerus internally and flex the elbow to 90 degrees. The insertion point is 2 cm (0.8 inches) above the surgical neck into the greater tubercle at a 45-degree angle to the front.
    - **Sternum:** The insertion point is 1 cm (0.3 inches) below the sternal notch.
- **Infants and neonates**
    - **Distal femur:** With the leg extended, the insertion point is 1 cm (0.3 inches) above and 1-2 cm (0.3-0.8 inches) medial to the patella.
    - **Proximal tibia:** The insertion point is 1-2 cm (0.3-0.8 inches) below and medial to the tibial tuberosity.
    - **Distal tibia:** The insertion point is 2 cm (0.8 inches) above the medial malleolus.

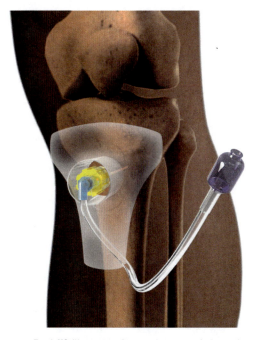

Fig-6-113. Illustration of intraosseous cannulation in the proximal tibia.

Technique

- Use an IO needle.
- Hold the IO needle perpendicular to the bone's surface at the identified landmark.
- Avoid the growth plate (epiphyseal plate) when performing the procedure in pediatric patients.
- Upon insertion, a distinct resistance or "hard stop" is encountered, indicating contact with the bone.
- Ensure that approximately 5 mm of the needle remains visible above the skin to confirm adequate penetration.
- Attach a syringe to draw bone marrow, verifying correct needle placement.
- Secure the needle firmly to avoid any potential dislodgement or bending during use.
- Avoid keeping IO access in place for more than 24 hours because prolonged use increases the risk of complications.

07

Scan the QR code for IV technique videos

IV ACCESS IN SPECIAL POPULATIONS

IV access in special populations refers to the considerations and adaptations healthcare professionals must make when placing IV lines in patients who do not fit the typical mold due to age, health conditions, or specific physiological circumstances.

7.1 IV access in pediatric patients

Securing venous access in infants and children presents unique challenges due to the delicate nature of their veins, potential dehydration, and anxiety about the procedure. This manual focuses primarily on IV access in adults. However, here are essential points to consider when attempting vein access in pediatric patients.

Smaller and fragile veins

- *Challenge:* The veins of pediatric patients are notably smaller and more fragile than those of adults, requiring extra care and precision during venipuncture.
- *Solution:* Choose the smallest IV gauge that meets the needs of the prescribed therapy to minimize discomfort and potential damage to veins.
- **Note:** Ultrasound can be used to aid the vein identification and cannulation. However, ultrasound-guided IV insertion is typically best reserved for challenging cases as it requires additional equipment, time, and expertise and is not suited for small, superficial veins, which is the case for most pediatric patients.

Movement concerns

- *Challenge:* Children frequently move during cannulation, which increases the risk of catheter dislodgement.
- *Solution:* In particularly challenging scenarios, such as with uncooperative children or patients with certain disabilities who require IV access, consider the administration of intramuscular ketamine (2-4 mg/kg). This creates a state of sedation and transient amnesia within approximately 5-10 minutes, providing a window of opportunity to insert a catheter or draw blood for analysis. Properly secure and stabilize the catheter after insertion, and consider using pediatric-specific securement devices to accommodate children's activity levels.

Discomfort

- *Challenge:* The process of IV insertion can be a source of significant discomfort and distress for children, complicating the procedure.
- *Solution:* Use soothing strategies such as offering infants pacifiers or distraction methods. Manage pain proactively by applying topical anesthetics to the intended insertion site to numb this area.

Vein selection

- *Challenge:* Determining the most suitable venipuncture site can be challenging due to children's smaller, less visible, or less palpable veins.
- *Solution:* Consider the more accessible scalp veins or foot veins in neonates.

Surface veins in neonates

- *Challenge:* In neonates and newborns, veins lie very close to the skin's surface, making them more susceptible to being punctured through and making venipuncture challenging.
- *Solution:* During insertion, maintain the needle at a very low, almost flat angle, nearly parallel to the skin. This technique allows for better control of the depth of needle entry, reducing the risk of puncturing the opposite vein wall or causing tissue trauma.

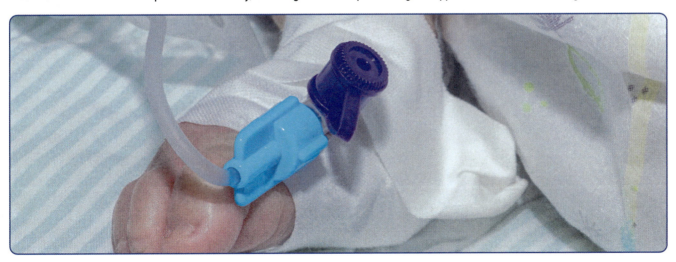

Fig-7-114. Foot veins may be used for IV access in pediatric patients as they may be more accessible than the standard peripheral veins in the arm or hand.

Step-by-step technique of IV cannulation in the hand of a pediatric patient

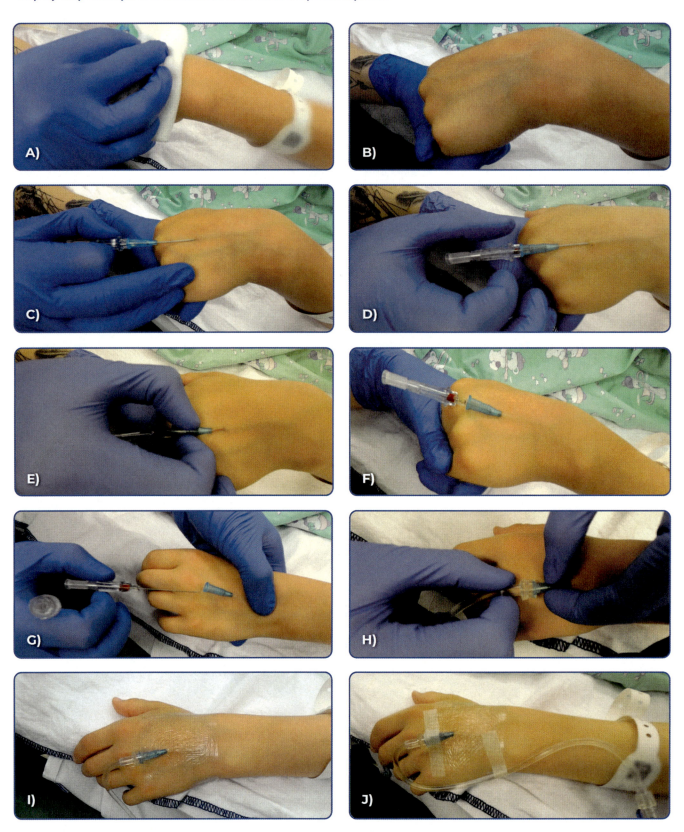

Fig-7-115. A) Disinfect the insertion site. B) Stabilize the veins in the hand and select a vein. C) Insert the needle at a shallow angle of 15-30 degrees relative to the skin. D) Blood in the flashback chamber indicates that the needle is inside the vein. E) Advance the catheter an additional 1-2 mm to ensure that the catheter tip is in the vein. F) Thread the catheter over the needle into the vein. G) Retract the needle. H) Attach the IV tubing to the catheter. I) Secure the catheter with an occlusive dressing. J) Loop the IV tubing and tape it to the skin away from the insertion site.

> **TIPS**
> - **Catheter size:** Select the optimal catheter gauge. A short 24G or 26G catheter is typically the best in pediatric patients. To put the flow rates in perspective, using a 24G IV in an infant is equivalent to using two 18G IVs in adults.
> - **Site preference:** The best anatomical IV insertion sites are often the back of the hand in children or feet in babies.
> - In babies and small children, securing a vein in the foot is often easier since the hand is more prone to movement. Transillumination is a valuable tool to pinpoint veins in the dorsum of the hand.
> - **Immobilize:** The key to successful IV insertion in infants is immobilizing the extremity where the IV is placed. The tendency of children to wiggle can render IV insertion nearly impossible.
> - **Use the free hand:** Use your free hand to stabilize the vein, pull the skin away, and immobilize the hand while starting an IV line with the other hand.

> Access the videos for this section by scanning the QR code at the beginning of the chapter.

Scalp vein cannulation

Scalp vein cannulation, often utilized in infants and young children, is an alternative for peripheral IV access when traditional venous access in the arms or legs is challenging. It can also be used in adults under similar circumstances.

Indications	Complications
· Neonates and infants	· Infection
· Dehydration	· Phlebitis
· Medication administration	· Extravasation
· Parenteral nutrition	· Occlusion
· Blood transfusion	· Hematoma
· Chemotherapy	· Air embolism
· Emergencies	· Scalp injury
	· Thrombosis

Here are some tips for effective scalp vein cannulation.

Patient preparation: Explain the procedure to parents or guardians and ensure the child is as comfortable as possible.

Patient position: Gently restrain the infant's head or ask an assistant to hold it steady. A calm, soothing environment helps in keeping the child relaxed.

Vein selection: Scalp veins are generally more prominent and accessible in neonates and infants. Choose a vein that appears straight and well-distended.

Use of a smaller gauge needle: Select a smaller gauge butterfly needle, which is more suitable for the scalp veins. Use a 24G or 26G butterfly needle to insert the IV catheter at a 20-30 degree angle.

Sterile technique: Clean the chosen site with an antiseptic solution and maintain an aseptic technique throughout the procedure.

Gentle insertion: Carefully insert the needle at a low angle, with the bevel facing up. The scalp's superficial veins require a delicate touch to avoid puncturing the vein.

Secure the cannula: Once in place, secure the needle with tape, ensuring it doesn't obstruct the child's movements or cause discomfort.

Use of protective covering: Consider using a soft, protective covering over the site to prevent accidental dislodgement.

Regular monitoring: Frequently check the IV site for signs of infiltration, infection, or phlebitis, especially since the pediatric patient may be unable to communicate discomfort effectively.

Pain management: Minimize discomfort during the procedure with appropriate pain management strategies.

Documentation: Record the procedure details including the cannulation site, the needle size, and any complications or patient reactions.

Parental guidance: Provide parents or guardians with information on how to care for the IV site and what signs of complications to look for.

Scalp vein cannulation requires skill and patience and should be performed by healthcare professionals experienced in pediatric IV therapy. The primary focus should always be on patient safety and comfort.

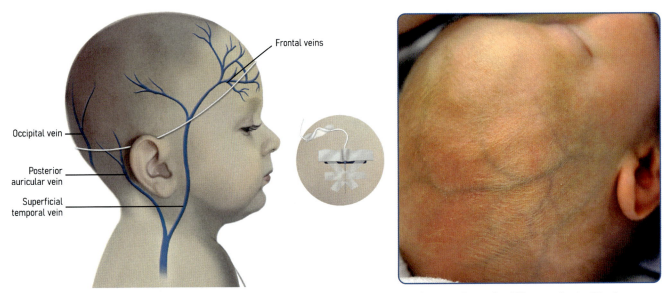

Fig-7-116. Scalp vein cannulation, often utilized in infants and young children, is an alternative for peripheral IV access when traditional venous access in the arms or legs is challenging.

7.2 IV access in elderly patients

Thinner skin and fragile veins
- *Challenge:* The skin in elderly patients tends to be thinner and more delicate, and the veins are more fragile and prone to bruising or tearing.
- *Solution:* Use smaller gauge catheters whenever possible and a vein stabilizer or vein viewer to assist.

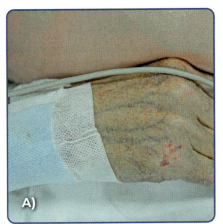 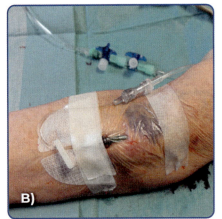 

Fig-7-117. A) Thin skin and fragile veins in elderly patients. B) Veins in elderly are prone to bruising. C) Dehydration and loss of elasticity of subcutaneous tissue complicate IV cannulation in elderly patients.

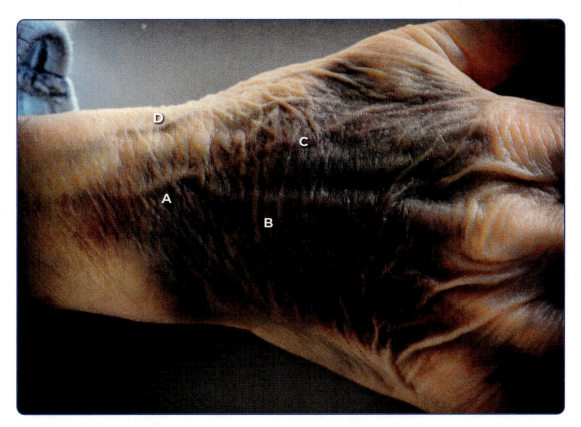

Fig-7-118. Example of thrombosed, overused peripheral veins that have become unusable (A, B, C). The vein over the lateral aspect of the proximal wrist (D) appears still usable, but has thickened wall, and requires a smaller gauge IV catheter (e.g. 22G), good stabilization and rapid (snake-bite) insertion for successful cannulation.

Decreased vein elasticity

- *Challenge:* Veins in the elderly may be sclerotic with hypertrophic walls, making them more difficult to stabilize (rolling veins) and more challenging for the needle to enter.
- *Solution:* Stabilize the vein with the non-dominant hand and use traction to maintain the vein in position.

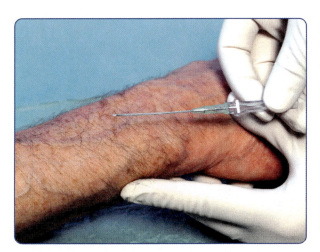

Fig-7-119. Stabilize the vein with the non-dominant hand and use digital traction with two fingers to maintain the vein in position.

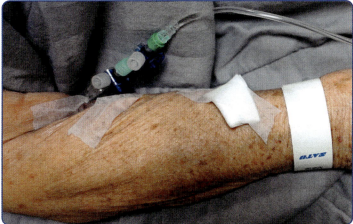

Fig-7-120. Administering an IV in an elderly patient can be challenging because of decreased skin turgor, reduced elasticity in connective tissues, and veins that are both fragile and prone to shifting. The combination of these factors often leads to multiple attempts.

Less visible and palpable veins

- *Challenge:* Diminished skin turgor or increased adipose tissue can obscure vein visibility and palpability.
- *Solution:* Use vein illumination technology or ultrasound guidance to select a vein. Keep the arm in a dependent position to encourage venous filling.

More frequent valves and tortuous veins

- *Challenge:* The greater prevalence of intricate valves and tortuous veins, coupled with connective tissue atrophy in elderly patients, complicates IV cannulation.
- *Solution:* Use palpation to identify venous valves and avoid them. Ultrasound guidance can assist in identifying deeper, more suitable veins.

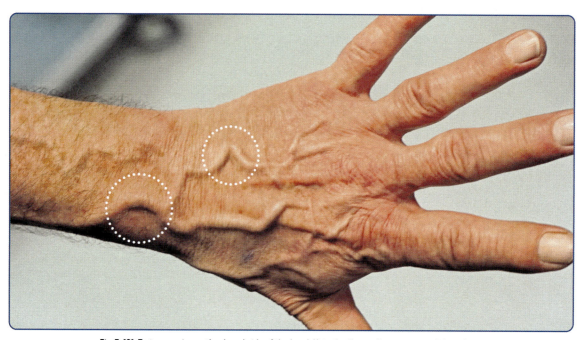

Fig-7-121. Tortuous veins on the dorsal side of the hand. Note the "bumpy" appearance of the valves.

History of multiple IV insertions

- *Challenge:* Previous IV cannulations can result in scar tissue, rendering some sites unsuitable for new insertions.
- *Solution:* Ask about previous IV sites and examine for scarred areas. Rotate sites when possible. Ask the patient where the IV works best for them. Many will point to where they previously had successful IVs.

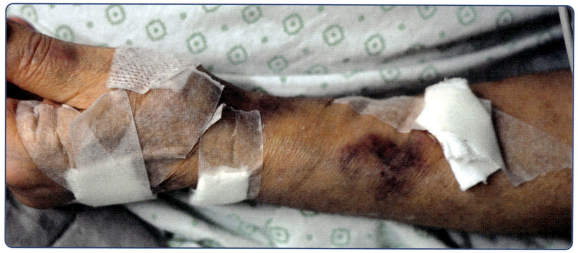

Fig-7-122. Multiple failed attempts at IV cannulation can result in sites being unsuitable for new insertions.

Decreased patient tolerance

- *Challenge:* Lower tolerance to multiple punctures in elderly patients may be due to increased sensitivity to pain, anxiety, or cognitive dysfunction.
- *Solution:* Use local anesthetic and distraction techniques as appropriate and maintain clear, reassuring communication to alleviate discomfort.

Risk of phlebitis

- *Challenge:* Phlebitis, an inflammation of the veins, can be a complication of IV therapy, and certain medications are known to have a higher risk of causing this condition. These medications can irritate the vein's inner lining, leading to inflammation and discomfort. Cumulative infusion of such medications and frequent IV cannulations can cause difficulties in future IV access.
- *Solution:* The risk of phlebitis can be reduced by proper dilution of medications, slow and steady infusion rates, and frequent rotation of IV sites. Using larger veins and ensuring proper IV catheter size and placement can also help minimize this risk. Always be vigilant for signs of phlebitis and take appropriate measures to prevent and manage it.

Some examples of medications that are commonly associated with the risk of phlebitis when administered intravenously include:

- **Vancomycin:** An antibiotic well-known for its potential to cause phlebitis. Infuse vancomycin slowly and dilute appropriately.
- **Potassium chloride:** Used to treat or prevent low potassium levels in the blood. High concentrations or rapid infusion of potassium chloride can be particularly irritating to veins.
- **Chemotherapy agents:** Many chemotherapeutic agents, such as doxorubicin and vincristine, are vesicants that can cause severe tissue damage if they leak from the vein. They can also cause phlebitis if infused too rapidly or in high concentrations.
- **Calcium supplements:** IV calcium (e.g. calcium gluconate) can be irritating to the vein walls, especially if infused rapidly.
- **Amiodarone:** Used for certain types of cardiac arrhythmias. Administer it through a central line to reduce the risk of phlebitis.
- **Diazepam (Valium):** Used for anxiety, seizures, and other conditions. It is known to be irritating to veins and can cause phlebitis.
- **Ciprofloxacin:** An antibiotic that, when given IV, can cause irritation to the veins.
- **Nafcillin:** An antibiotic used to treat bacterial infections, a frequent cause of phlebitis.

Other effects of various medications

The cumulative effects of various medications can further make IV cannulation challenging for the elderly. Here are some medications to be aware of. While immediate changes in an acute setting might not be feasible, understanding the mechanisms behind the effects of these commonly prescribed medications can provide valuable insight.

Anticoagulants

- *Examples:* Warfarin, heparin, dabigatran, apixaban, rivaroxaban.
- *Challenge:* Extended bleeding times complicate the post-insertion phase.
- *Solution:* Apply firm pressure post-insertion to prevent excessive hematomas hindering future cannulation attempts.

Antiplatelet agents

- *Examples:* Aspirin, clopidogrel.
- *Challenge:* Increased bleeding and hematoma risks.
- *Solution:* Monitor the insertion site closely for signs of prolonged bleeding.

Diuretics

- *Examples:* Furosemide, hydrochlorothiazide.
- *Challenge:* May cause dehydration, resulting in less visible veins.
- *Solution:* Assess hydration status before cannulation, and if necessary, hydrate the patient to enhance vein visibility.

Vasodilators

- *Examples:* Nifedipine, amlodipine, hydralazine.
- *Challenge:* Long-term use may modify vein tone and responsiveness.
- *Solution:* Be aware of potential vein behavior alterations during cannulation.

Steroids

- *Examples:* Prednisolone, cortisone.
- *Challenge:* Prolonged use might result in skin thinning, increasing the risk of skin tearing, though they may also cause fluid retention, which could influence vein condition.
- *Solution:* Proceed cautiously during cannulation and thoroughly assess the skin and vein condition.

Access the videos for this section by scanning the QR code at the beginning of the chapter.

Step-by-step technique of IV cannulation in the hand of an elderly patient demonstrating the difficulties with frail veins

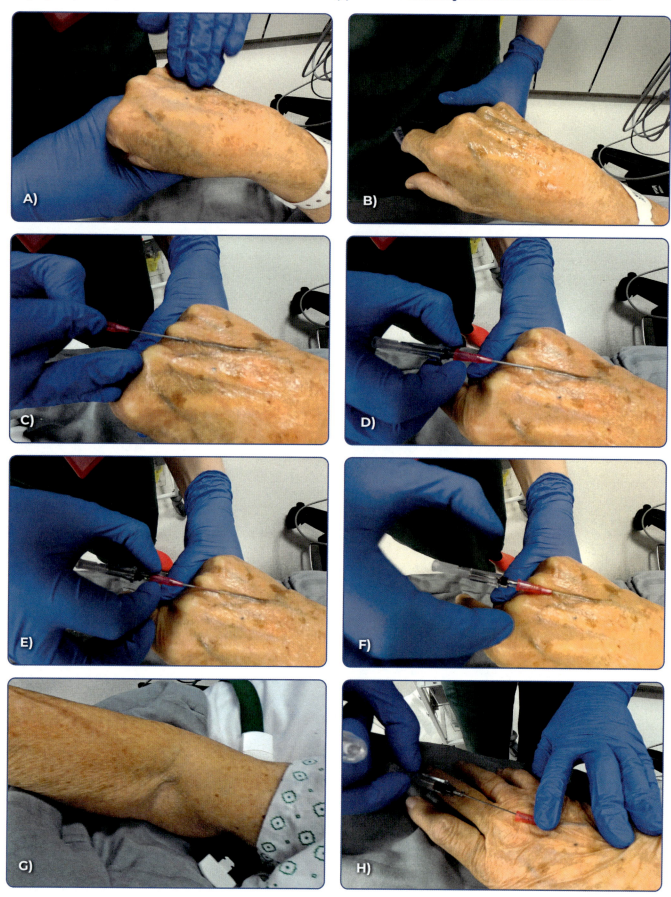

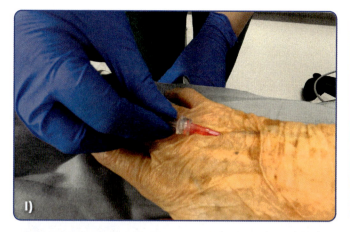
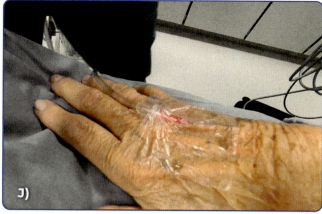
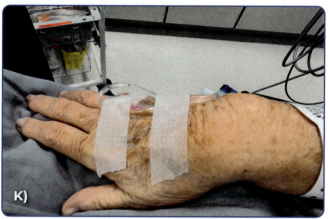

Fig-7-123. A) Lightly tap the skin to accomplish mild vasodilation to increase vein visibility. B) Disinfect the insertion site. C) Stabilize the hand and insert the needle at a shallow angle of ≤ 15 degrees. D) Advance the needle to ensure that the needle is in the vein. E) Blood in the flashback chamber indicates the needle is inside the vein. F) Advance the catheter an additional 1-2 mm to ensure the catheter tip is in the vein. G) Release the tourniquet. H) Retract the needle. I) Attach the IV tubing to the catheter. J) Secure the catheter with an occlusive dressing. K) Loop the IV tubing and tape it to the skin away from the insertion site.

TIPS

- Carefully tighten the tourniquet, as fragile veins can easily rupture at sites of previous attempts. Consider using a blood pressure cuff in a venostasis mode instead to achieve a more regulated and evenly distributed pressure.
- Older people tend to have more superficial veins with less supportive connective tissue. Lower the angle of the needle during insertion to prevent the needle from puncturing the vein's wall (through and through).

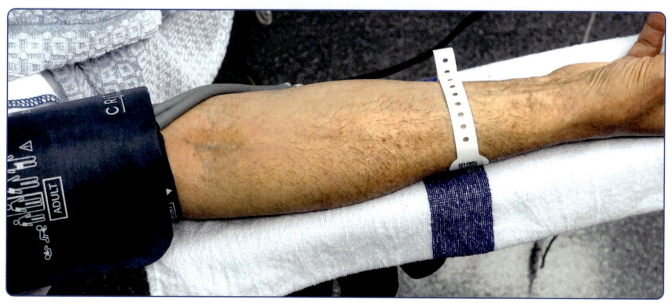

Fig-7-124. Using a blood pressure cuff as a tourniquet during venipuncture in elderly patients.

7.3 IV access in underweight patients

IV access in patients with low body weight or a low body mass index (BMI) presents unique challenges for healthcare professionals. These individuals often have less subcutaneous fat and smaller, more fragile veins, making traditional IV insertion more difficult and increasing the risk of complications such as vein damage or infiltration. The reduced vein visibility and palpability require a higher level of skill and sometimes necessitate the use of ultrasound-guided techniques to achieve successful venipuncture. Additionally, these patients may have a higher risk of adverse reactions from fluid overload or medication toxicity, necessitating careful monitoring and adjustment of IV fluid and medication dosages.

Here's a brief overview of the challenges and solutions to IV access in underweight patients.

Superficial and fragile veins
- *Challenge:* While more superficial, veins can be fragile and prone to collapse.
- *Solution:* Choose a smaller gauge needle to reduce vein trauma during venipuncture. Make sure to stabilize the vein before insertion.

Prominent bony landmarks
- *Challenge:* The prominence of bony structures can make it difficult to stabilize the extremity and find a suitable vein.
- *Solution:* Use padding or soft supports to provide comfort and secure the extremities. If necessary, explore alternative venous sites.

Reduced venous volume
- *Challenge:* Decreased total body volume might result in smaller, less distensible veins.
- *Solution:* Hydrate the patient if appropriate and feasible. Consider using ultrasound guidance to optimize vein selection and reduce the number of puncture attempts.

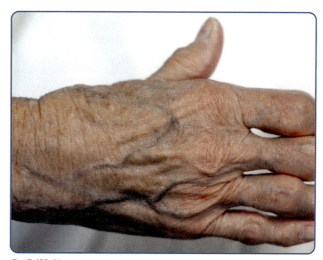

Fig-7-125. IV access in underweight patients can be challenging due to loss of connective tissue and frail veins, as is the case in this elderly patient with low BMI and osteoarthritis.

Risk of hematoma formation
- *Challenge:* The delicate nature of the veins and surrounding tissues can increase the risk of hematoma formation in underweight patients.
- *Solution:* Apply gentle pressure immediately after venipuncture and secure the catheter well to minimize post-insertion bleeding. Regularly assess the IV site for signs of hematoma.

7.4 IV access in obese patients

Securing IV access in obese patients presents a unique set of challenges for healthcare professionals. The increasing prevalence of obesity worldwide has made this a common issue in clinical settings, necessitating a deeper understanding and specialized approaches to ensure effective venous cannulation. In obese individuals, the excessive adipose tissue can obscure superficial veins, making them difficult to palpate and visualize. This complicates the identification of suitable veins for cannulation and increases the risk of multiple cannulation attempts, leading to patient discomfort and potential complications such as hematoma, infection, or thrombophlebitis.

The anatomical and physiological alterations associated with obesity, including changes in blood vessel elasticity and the potential for deeper vein locations, require clinicians to adapt their techniques and equipment. For instance, using longer and larger gauge needles may be necessary to access deeper veins successfully. Additionally, advanced technologies such as ultrasound-guided IV access have become invaluable tools in overcoming the visualization challenges posed by obesity.

Given these complexities, healthcare providers must possess a high level of skill and patience, and understand the specific considerations and adaptations required for IV access in obese patients. This includes not only technical adjustments but also a compassionate approach that acknowledges the potential for increased anxiety and discomfort experienced by obese patients during venous cannulation. Addressing these challenges effectively is essential for delivering high-quality care and ensuring the safety and comfort of obese patients requiring IV therapy.

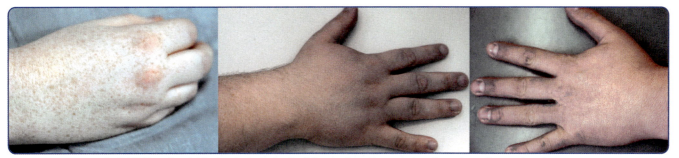

Fig-7-126. Examples of difficult veins in the hands of obese patients. The excessive adipose tissue obscures the veins.

Excess adipose tissue

- *Challenge:* Excess adipose tissue can obscure veins (e.g., veins on the dorsum of the hand and the deep brachial vein), complicating palpation and access.
- *Solution:* Ultrasound-guided IV insertion may be advantageous for identifying deeper veins and enhancing first-attempt success. Choose a longer catheter for proper vein access.

Diverse venous sites

- *Challenge:* Traditional venous access sites might be less feasible in obese patients.
- *Solution:* Explore alternative sites like the wrist's inner side (i.e., volar aspect) and the cephalic vein between the deltoid and pectoral muscles. Prominent veins can often be found over the shoulders, upper torso, or breasts of obese patients. While not ideal for prolonged infusions, these sites can offer immediate, temporary access using a small-gauge IV. Following hydration, more conventional venous sites may become more accessible.

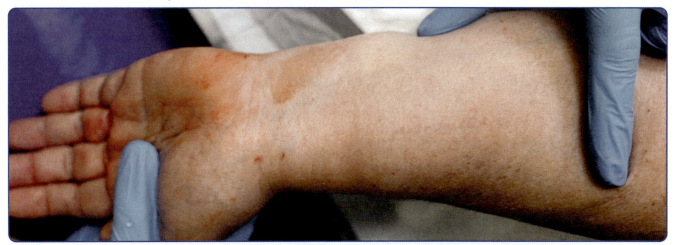

Fig-7-127. Alternative sites like the wrist's inner side (i.e., volar aspect) can be used when traditional venous access sites are not feasible.

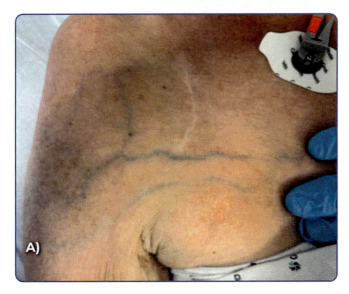

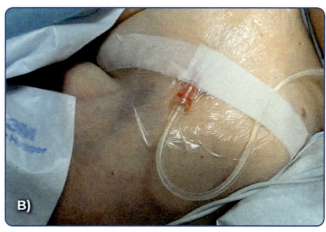

Fig-7-128. A) Prominent superficial chest veins are suitable for emergency cannulation in patients with difficult venous access in the upper or lower extremities. B) IV cannulation in the shoulder of an obese patient.

IV cannulation of a shoulder vein in an obese patient

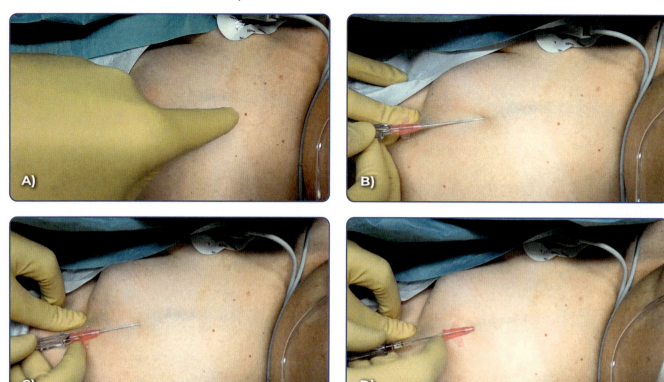

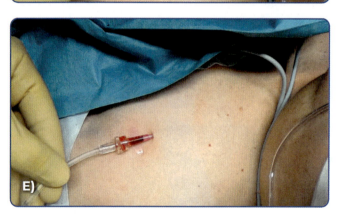

Fig-7-129. A) Example of a shoulder vein suitable for cannulation. B) Insert the needle at a shallow angle of 10 to 30 degrees relative to the skin. C) Appearance of blood in the flashback chamber. D) Thread the catheter over the needle into the vein, advance the needle-catheter system into the vein, and retract the needle. E) Attach the IV tubing to the catheter.

Venous access sites like the chest and shoulder veins should be reserved only for situations where other, more conventional sites are unavailable.

Risk of complications
- *Challenge:* The adipose tissue increases the likelihood of infiltration or extravasation of IV fluid.
- *Solution:* Frequently assess the IV site for early signs of infiltration and secure the catheter to reduce the chances of movement and displacement.

> Access the videos for this section by scanning the QR code at the beginning of the chapter.

7.5 IV access in patients with burns

Depending on their severity and location, burns can significantly alter the anatomy of the skin and underlying tissues, complicating the identification and cannulation of peripheral veins.

The presence of burns, especially in extensive cases, may limit traditional access sites and require healthcare professionals to employ alternative strategies and sites for cannulation. The integrity of the skin, the extent of tissue damage, and the potential for edema and vascular compromise are critical factors that influence the approach to IV access in burn patients.

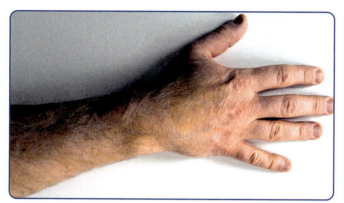
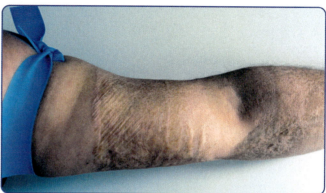
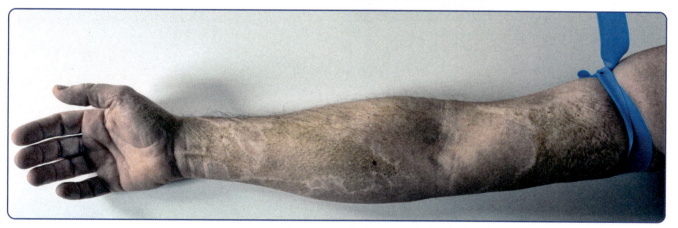

Fig-7-130. The presence of burns may complicate IV access due to excessive scars.

Here are the challenges and solutions for establishing IV access in patients with burns where the skin and subcutaneous tissue scars make IV access challenging.

Damaged skin and tissue

- *Challenge:* Burns can result in extensive skin and tissue damage, often limiting the availability of suitable IV access sites.
- *Solution:* Identify unburned or minimally damaged skin areas for potential IV insertion. For severe burns over large body areas, consider alternative access such as central lines, peripherally inserted central catheters, or IO cannulation.

Infection risk

- *Challenge:* Burn wounds provide a favorable environment for bacterial growth, increasing the risk of local and systemic infections.
- *Solution:* Follow strict aseptic methods during IV initiation. Regularly inspect the IV site for signs of infection and ensure that dressings are kept sterile, dry, and intact. For IV lines traversing burn tissue (i.e., eschar), establish a protocol for frequent replacement, ideally every 72 hours, to prevent potential colonization and infection.

Fluid shifts and edema

- *Challenge:* Burns can induce substantial fluid shifts, leading to edema, which might mask veins and complicate IV placement.
- *Solution:* Establish IV access as early as possible before edema occurs. Elevate affected limbs to reduce edema. Consider using ultrasound guidance to assist in visualizing veins beneath the swollen tissue.

Pain and discomfort

- *Challenge:* Patients with burns often experience intense pain, making any intervention, including IV insertion, more challenging and uncomfortable.
- *Solution:* Administer analgesics before attempting IV access or changing dressings.

Altered skin integrity

- *Challenge:* Burned skin may not hold adhesive tapes and dressings effectively, making catheter securement difficult.
- *Solution:* Choose burn-specific dressings or non-adhesive stabilizing devices. Consider suturing or stapling catheters to the skin. Regularly check the stability of the IV line to prevent dislodgement.

7.6 IV access in patients with diabetes

Patients with diabetes often have complications such as peripheral vascular disease, changes in skin texture, and susceptibility to infection, all of which can complicate the process of obtaining and maintaining reliable IV access.

The significance of understanding these challenges cannot be overstated, as IV access is essential for administering medications, fluids, and sometimes insulin, especially in acute care settings or during surgical procedures. The altered vascular integrity found in many diabetic patients, combined with potential edema and neuropathy, necessitates a strategic approach to cannulation, often requiring the use of ultrasound guidance, to improve success rates and minimize patient discomfort.

Vascular complications

- *Challenge:* Chronic hyperglycemia can lead to narrowed, hardened, or less elastic veins.
- *Solution:* Use ultrasound guidance to identify more robust veins. Consider deeper veins if superficial veins are compromised.

Skin changes and infections

- *Challenge:* Diabetes often alters skin texture, reduces the healing processes, and heightens infection susceptibility.
- *Solution:* Follow strict aseptic techniques during venipuncture to mitigate infection risks. Choose insertion sites free of skin changes or abnormalities.

Neuropathy and sensation change

- *Challenge:* Diabetic neuropathy may alter pain perception.
- *Solution:* Communicate clearly with the patient to understand their comfort level. Use local anesthetics judiciously to maintain patient comfort.

Fluid and electrolyte imbalances

- *Challenge:* Diabetic patients may present with dehydration or other fluid and electrolyte imbalances that can make veins less filled and more difficult to cannulate.
- *Solution:* Orally hydrate the patient to enhance venous volume and distensibility. Monitor the patient's electrolyte status and adjust care accordingly.

Thickened skin or scar tissue

- *Challenge:* Repeated insulin injections can lead to thickened skin or scar tissue areas, which may interfere with IV placement.
- *Solution:* Avoid areas of lipohypertrophy or thickened skin when selecting an IV site. Rotate IV sites and educate diabetic patients on rotating their injection sites to prevent skin complications.

Step-by-step technique of a double IV cannulation in a diabetic patient

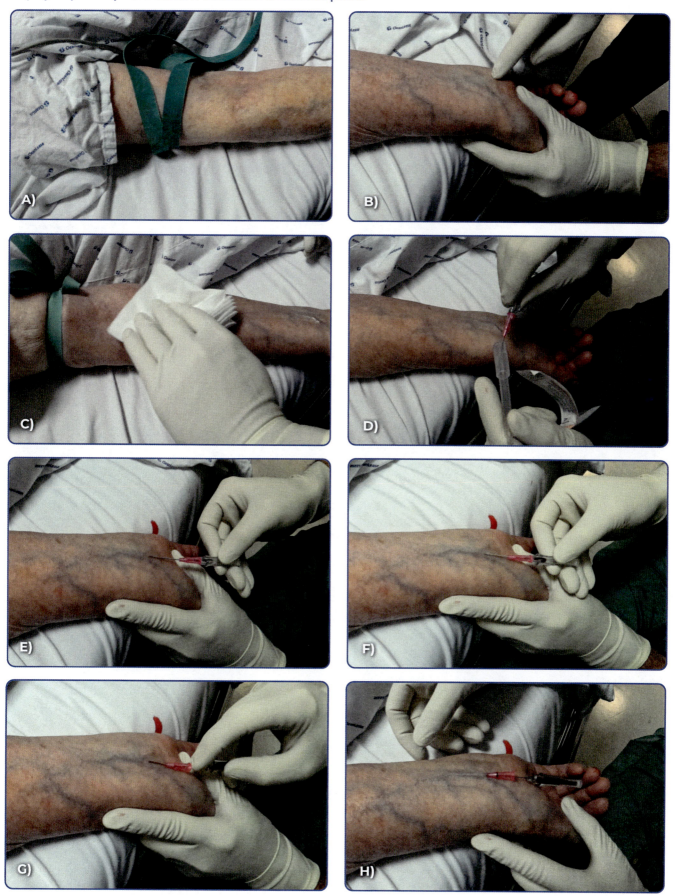

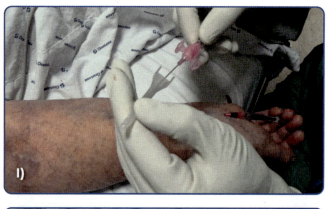
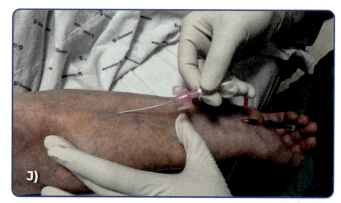
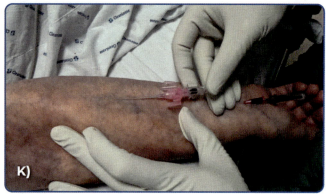
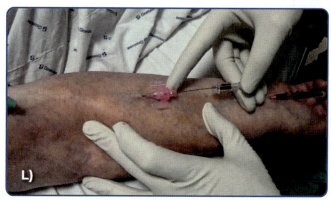
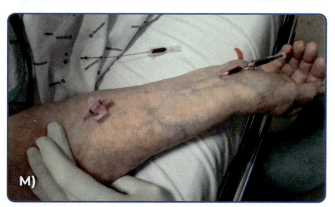
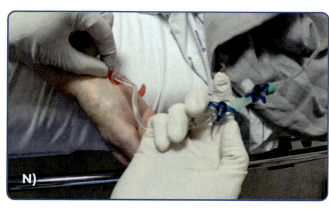
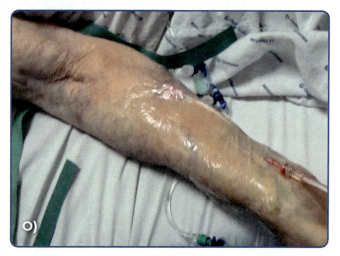

Fig-7-131. Double IV access in a patient with diabetes who required two IV lines for infusion of IV fluids for volume resuscitation and infusion of antibiotics. Note the tortuous and sclerotic appearance of the superficial veins in the patient's forearm. A) Apply the tourniquet. B) Identify suitable veins for IV cannulation. C) Disinfect the skin to make the veins more prominent. D) Use a bent and short 20G catheter. E) Stabilize the hand and insert the needle with a low angle. F) Look out for the blood flashback. G) Advance the catheter. H) One workable IV cannulation is established. I) Use a bent and winged 20G catheter to establish the second IV access point. J) Stabilize the arm and insert the needle with a very low angle. K) Look out for the blood flashback. L) Advance the catheter and retract the needle. M) A proximal and distal IV access point. N) Attach the IV tubing. O) Secure the catheter with adhesive dressing.

Access the videos for this section by scanning the QR code at the beginning of the chapter.

7.7 IV access in patients with a history of IV drug use

Patients with a history of IV drug use often present unique challenges when establishing IV access. Adopt an empathetic approach and utilize technical solutions to establish IV access in these patients.

> **NOTES**
> Many of these patients can provide valuable feedback regarding the best IV sites, what worked in the past, where the most accessible veins are, and so on.

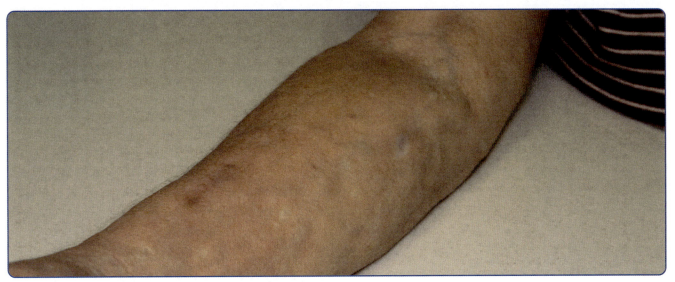

Fig-7-132. Arm of a patient with a history of IV drug use.

Here are some challenges to remember for these patients.

Damaged veins
- *Challenge:* Frequent IV drug use can severely damage veins, leading to thrombophlebitis or scarred and collapsed veins, complicating traditional IV access.
- *Solution:* Use ultrasound guidance to identify viable veins in non-traditional areas, as common sites might be overused or damaged. Consider alternative access methods, such as CVCs or IO access.

Infection risk
- *Challenge:* Precaution: increased risk of bloodborne infections such as HIV or hepatitis.
- *Solution:* Use standard precautions and personal protective equipment to avert transmission. Regularly screen for and manage infectious complications.

Soft tissue infections
- *Challenge:* Non-sterile IV drug use can introduce pathogens, giving rise to cellulitis, abscesses, or more severe infections.
- *Solution:* Avoid placing IV lines near infected areas, treat infections promptly, and consider alternative sites for IV access.

Withdrawal symptoms
- *Challenge:* Patients with active drug dependency may undergo withdrawal symptoms, complicating their care.
- *Solution:* Remain vigilant and prepared to address withdrawal manifestations or facilitate referrals to specialized care providers.

Trust issues
- *Challenge:* Patients may be distrustful due to previous negative experiences with healthcare providers or the stigma associated with drug use.
- *Solution:* Approach these patients with empathy and patience, working to build trust. Engage in open communication, provide reassurance, and use short-acting anxiolytic medications if necessary.

7.8 IV access in patients with a history of cancer or chemotherapy treatment

Patients with a history of cancer, especially those who have received chemotherapy, often experience venous changes that make IV access difficult. Chemotherapy agents can cause venous damage, leading to sclerosis, reduced elasticity, and increased fragility of the veins. Additionally, repeated venipunctures throughout the treatment can further compromise venous integrity, resulting in limited or difficult-to-access venous sites.

Fragile veins
- *Challenge:* Chemotherapy often causes veins to become fragile, making them prone to damage during IV insertion.
- *Solution:* Apply gentle techniques and use smaller gauge needles to minimize vein damage.

Limited access sites
- *Challenge:* Frequent IV therapies may have exhausted accessible peripheral veins.
- *Solution:* Evaluate the patient's history thoroughly and select alternative sites. Use ultrasound guidance to visualize suitable veins. Consider using midline catheters, PICCs, or CVCs.

Reduced immunity and infection risk
- *Challenge:* Cancer and chemotherapy may compromise the immune system, increasing the risk of infections.
- *Solution:* Employ strict aseptic techniques during IV insertion and maintenance. Check cannulation sites frequently for signs of infection and react promptly.

Tissue changes and sensitivity
- *Challenge:* Some chemotherapy medications can cause tissue changes, making the skin more sensitive or leading to extravasation injuries.
- *Solution:* Handle the skin carefully. Opt for smaller gauge needles, and check cannulation sites frequently for signs of leakage or injury.

Fluid overload
- *Challenge:* Certain cancer treatments may induce fluid retention, complicating the administration of additional IV fluids.
- *Solution:* Carefully calculate and monitor the volume of IV fluids administered to prevent fluid overload.

> **NOTES**
> - Advanced techniques, such as ultrasound-guided IV or central venous access may be necessary for identifying viable veins and achieving successful cannulation in patients with compromised venous access.
> - In some patients surgical intervention may be needed to establish permanent access to the circulation for repeated chemotherapy treatment.

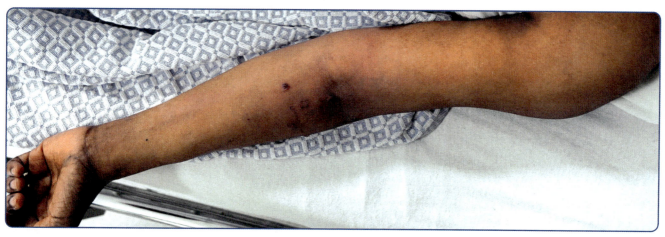

Fig-7-133. Overused veins with skin discoloration due to irradiation in a patient with cancer.

7.9 IV access in emergency settings

Emergency situations demand swift action; obtaining IV access can be the difference between life and death. However, the process is fraught with difficulty, especially in patients with compromised vascular access due to dehydration, trauma, shock, obesity, or IV drug use. We introduce a practical algorithm specifically designed for IV access in emergency settings to streamline the decision-making process and enhance clinical outcomes. These algorithms are step-by-step guides that address initial site selection, techniques for difficult IV access, use of ultrasound-guided venipuncture, and alternative access methods such as IO infusion. It is intended to serve as a practical tool for clinicians, reducing the time to achieve access and improving patient care.

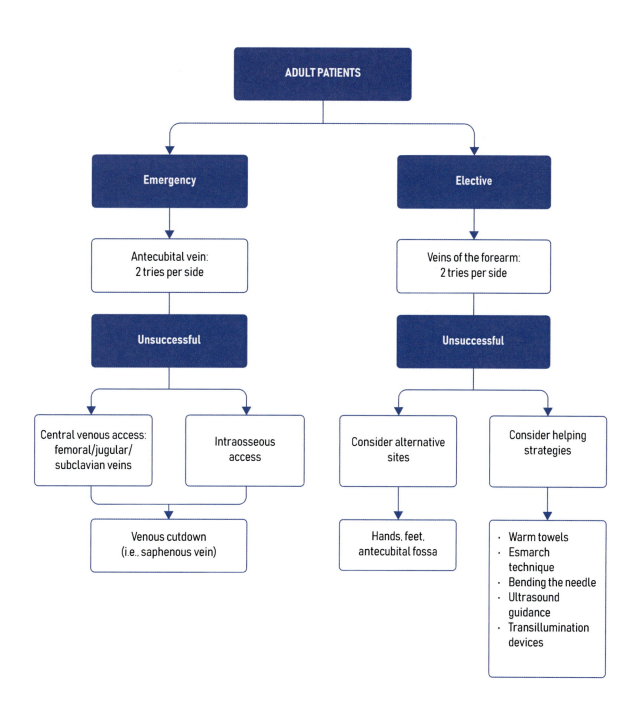

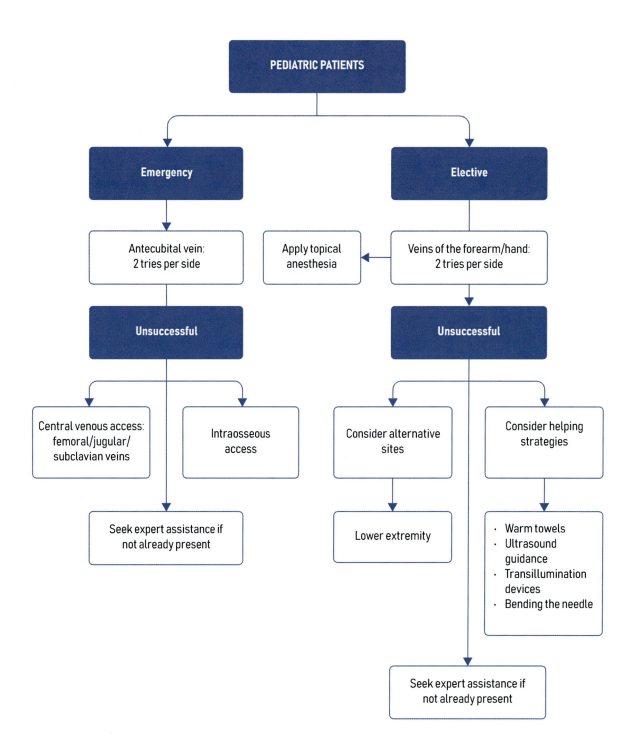

These algorithms emphasize a systematic approach, starting with the least invasive methods and progressing to more advanced techniques if initial attempts fail. They consider patient-specific factors and encourage clinicians to use clinical judgment and patient assessment to guide their choice of technique.

08

Scan the QR code for IV technique videos

COMPLICATIONS OF IV CANNULATION

IV cannulation is a standard procedure in healthcare, but like all medical procedures, it carries the risk of complications. With knowledge and care, many complications can be prevented or effectively managed.

8.1 Phlebitis and thrombophlebitis

Phlebitis and thrombophlebitis are two common complications associated with IV therapy. Phlebitis refers to the inflammation of a vein, while thrombophlebitis involves the formation of a blood clot within the inflamed vein (typically in the legs). Thrombophlebitis associated with IV therapy is a significant concern in clinical practice, affecting patient comfort, treatment duration, and overall outcomes.

Causes: Vein irritation may stem from mechanical factors such as needle trauma or catheter friction or extended use, chemical irritants from administered medications, or bacterial contamination caused by poor sterilization methods when starting or managing an IV line.

Signs & symptoms: Redness and warmth over the vein, tenderness or pain, swelling, a palpable cord indicating thrombus formation, and fever in case of a systemic infection.

Effects: Thrombophlebitis can progress to a local infection, cellulitis, or even venous thromboembolism, resulting in a risk of pulmonary embolism.

Treatment: Discontinue and remove the IV, apply a warm or cold compress to ease the pain, and consider anti-inflammatory medication, antibiotic therapy, and anticoagulation in case of thrombus formation. Establish another IV access at a different site if continuous IV therapy is required.

Prevention: Maintain a proper aseptic technique, select the appropriate catheter size, and rotate IV insertion sites regularly.

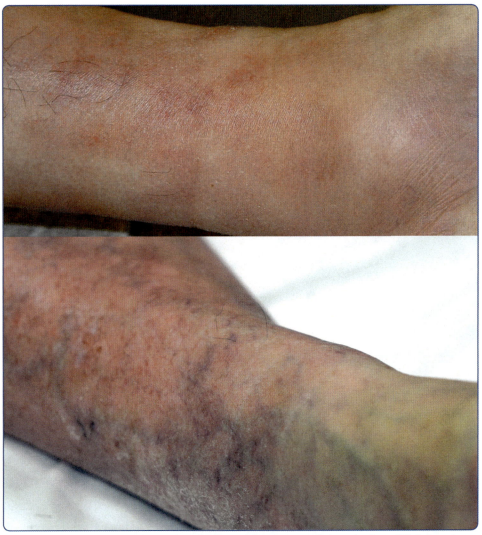

Fig-8-134. Thrombophlebitis after indwelling saphenous vein cannulation and prolonged IV infusion.

PHLEBITIS & THROMBOPHLEBITIS

CAUSES
- Mechanical irritation
  - Needle or catheter friction
  - Extended use of catheter
- Chemical irritation from administered medications
- Infection due to bacterial contamination

SIGNS & SYMPTOMS
- Redness over the vein
- Warmth over the vein
- Tenderness or pain
- Swelling
- A palpable cord indicating a thrombus
- Fever

EFFECTS
- Can progress to:
  - A local infection
  - Cellulitis
  - Venous thromboembolism
    → pulmonary embolism

TREATMENT
- Discontinue and remove the IV
- Apply a warm or cold compress to ease the pain
- Consider
  - Anti-inflammatory medication
  - Antibiotics
  - Anticoagulation in case of thrombus formation
- Establish another IV access at a different site if continuous IV therapy is required

PREVENTION
- Maintain a proper aseptic technique
- Select the appropriate catheter size
- Check the IV site regularly for signs of irritation or infection
- Rotate IV insertion sites regularly

8.2 Infiltration

Infiltration is a common complication of IV therapy, occurring when non-vesicant fluids or medications inadvertently enter the surrounding tissue instead of the vein. This mishap can happen during the administration of IV fluids, leading to a range of symptoms from mild discomfort to severe tissue damage, depending on the volume and nature of the infiltrated substance.

Causes: Poor vein selection, improper cannula placement, vein perforation, or cannula dislodgement due to frequent movements.

Signs & symptoms: Swelling, discomfort, burning, or tightness around the IV site, coolness and paleness of the skin.

Effects: Mild infiltration causes localized swelling and discomfort, while severe cases or vesicants lead to tissue necrosis, blistering, scarring, or loss of function.

Treatment: Discontinue and remove the IV, elevate the affected limb to drain the infiltrate, and apply a warm compress to cause vasodilation or a cold compress to reduce swelling. Establish another IV access at a different site if continuous IV therapy is required.

Prevention: Ensure proper IV placement, secure it properly, and check its position frequently.

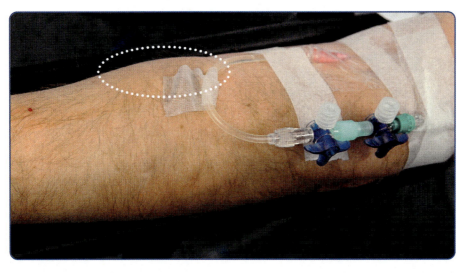

Fig-8-135. Infiltration of an IV infusion catheter in the forearm. The IV has been removed and a new site has been successfully cannulated.

INFILTRATION

CAUSES
- Poor vein selection
- Improper cannula placement
- Vein perforation
- Cannula dislodgement
- Frequent movements
- Too short IV catheter
- Inadequate securing of IV catheter

SIGNS & SYMPTOMS
- Swelling
- Discomfort
- Burning around the IV site
- Tightness around the IV site
- Pain at the IV site
- Coolness and paleness of the skin

EFFECTS
- Mild infiltration
  - Localized swelling
  - Localized discomfort
- Severe infiltration
  - Tissue necrosis
  - Blistering
  - Scarring
  - Loss of function

TREATMENT
- Discontinue and remove
- Elevate the affected limb to drain the infiltrate
- Apply a warm compress to cause vasodilation or a cold compress to reduce swelling
- Establish another IV access at a different site if continuous IV therapy is required

PREVENTION
- Ensure proper IV placement
- Secure the IV properly
- Check the position of the IV frequently

8.3 Extravasation

IV extravasation is similar to infiltration and demands immediate attention. Depending on the type of solution or medication that has extravasated, it can range from a minor irritation to a severe complication. The severity of the injury can vary widely, from simple skin irritation to more significant tissue damage, including necrosis. This variability is mainly dependent on the vesicant properties of the substance involved.

Causes: Similar to infiltration: Improper cannula placement, vein perforation, cannula dislodgement, or high pressure during infusion.

Signs & symptoms: Swelling, pain, redness at the infusion site, burning or stinging sensation, blistering, and tissue necrosis.

Effects: Severe extravasation can lead to grafting or even amputation.

Treatment: Stop the infusion and administer the antidote through the same IV. Further intervention may involve the application of a cold or warm compress, massage and an elastic bandage, elevation of the affected limb, and potential use of hyaluronidase (helps to absorb the extravasated fluid). In cases of severe tissue damage, surgical intervention may be required.

Prevention: Effective vein evaluation before cannulation, appropriate choice of cannula size, and secure fixation to avoid displacement are essential. Consistent monitoring of the IV site and infusion rate is crucial, and utilizing a central line over a peripheral line for known vesicants, when suitable, can further mitigate risks.

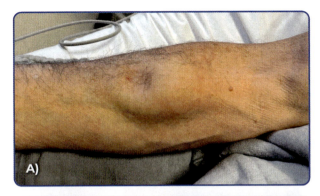
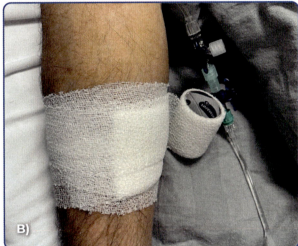

Fig-8-136. A) Extravasation of IV fluid. B) Treatment consists of massage and an elastic bandage.

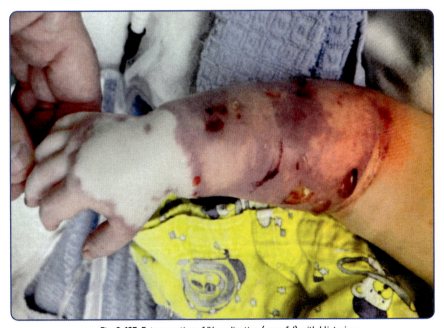

Fig-8-137. Extravasation of IV medication (propofol) with blistering.

EXTRAVASATION

CAUSES
- Improper cannula placement
- Vein perforation
- Cannula dislodgement
- Prolonged IV use
- High pressure infusion
- Multiple attempts at venipuncture

SIGNS & SYMPTOMS
- Swelling
- Pain
- Redness at the infusion site
- Burning or stinging sensation
- Blistering
- Tissue necrosis

EFFECTS
- Grafting
- Amputation

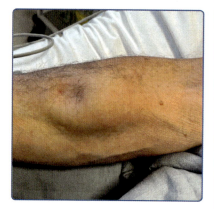

TREATMENT
- Stop the infusion
- Administer the antidote through the same IV (if applicable)
- Elevate the affected limb to drain the infiltrate
- Apply a warm compress to cause vasodilation or a cold compress to reduce swelling
- Massage and apply a bandage
- Consider hyaluronidase (helps to absorb the extravasated fluid)
- Consider surgical intervention to release compartment syndrome

PREVENTION
- Evaluate the vein before cannulation
- Choose an appropriate cannula size and lengths
- Secure the IV to avoid displacement
- Frequently monitor the IV site and infusion rate
- Utilize a central line over a peripheral line for known vesicants

8.4 Hematoma

A hematoma is a collection of blood outside of blood vessels caused by a leakage or rupture of the vessel wall. In the context of IV access, it occurs when the needle injures a vein, leading to blood accumulating in the surrounding tissue. Hematomas can vary in size and may present as visible bruising, swelling, or a palpable lump near the IV site.

Causes: The development of a hematoma during IV access can be attributed to several factors, including:

- **Technique-related issues:** Improper needle insertion angle, excessive force use, or failure to stabilize the vein can damage the vessel.
- **Patient-related factors:** Conditions that affect blood clotting, such as hemophilia or anticoagulant therapy, increase the risk. Fragile or small veins, commonly seen in the elderly or patients with chronic illness, also pose a higher risk.
- **Equipment-related issues:** The use of needles or catheters that are too large for the selected vein can contribute to vessel injury.

Signs & symptoms: Immediate swelling, bruising, and tenderness around the IV insertion site.

Effects: A large hematoma can cause significant pain, compress nerves, limit joint mobility, and, in rare cases, cause compartment syndrome.

Treatment: Remove the IV, apply a cold pack, elevate the affected area, and monitor the patient for any signs of compartment syndrome.

Prevention: Use the correct technique for venipuncture, ensure the vein is punctured only once by the needle, and apply sufficient pressure after removing the needle.

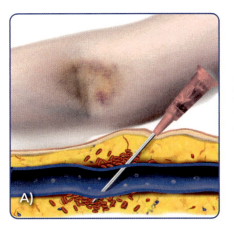
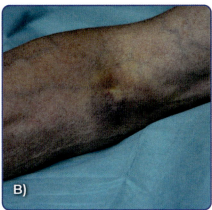

Fig-8-138. A) Illustration of hematoma formation. B) Hematoma formation in the arm. C) Swelling caused by a hematoma in the hand.

HEMATOMA

CAUSES
- Puncture of the back wall of the vein
- Accidental catheter dislodgement
- Fragile veins
- Repeated attempts at cannulation
- No pressure applied after removal of the cannula

SIGNS & SYMPTOMS
- Swelling
- Bruising
- Tenderness around the IV site
- Discoloration

EFFECTS
- Pain
- Compression of nerves
- Limited joint mobility
- Compartment syndrome

TREATMENT
- Remove the IV
- Elevate the affected limb
- Apply a cold compress to reduce swelling
- Monitor the patient for any signs of compartment syndrome

PREVENTION
- Use the correct technique for venipuncture
- Select an appropriate vein
- Limit puncture attempts
- Apply sufficient pressure after removing the needle

8.5 IV-associated infection

IV catheter-associated infections are a group of infections that can occur at the catheter insertion site or within the bloodstream, related to the use of an IV catheter. These infections can range from localized skin infections to more severe conditions like phlebitis, septic thrombophlebitis, and catheter-related bloodstream infections. The severity and type of infection depend on various factors, including the catheter's location, the patient's health status, and the presence of pathogenic organisms.

Pathogenesis: The pathogenesis of catheter-associated infections involves the colonization of the catheter surface by microorganisms, which can originate from the patient's skin, the hands of healthcare providers, or contaminated equipment. These microorganisms can form biofilms on the catheter, making them resistant to antibiotics and the immune system, thereby complicating treatment and increasing the risk of systemic infection.

Causes: Contamination during IV insertion or through contaminated fluids or equipment, improper hand hygiene, or the prolonged use of an IV site.

Signs & symptoms: Redness, warmth, swelling, tenderness at the IV site, purulent discharge, and the formation of an abscess. A systemic infection (i.e., sepsis) can present with fever, chills, hypotension, tachycardia, confusion, and an increased white blood cell count.

Effects: Local infection can progress to deep tissue infections and bacteremia, potentially leading to sepsis.

Treatment: Remove the IV catheter, clean the insertion site, apply topical treatments, and administer appropriate antibiotics.

Prevention: Maintain a strict aseptic technique and frequently assess the IV site.

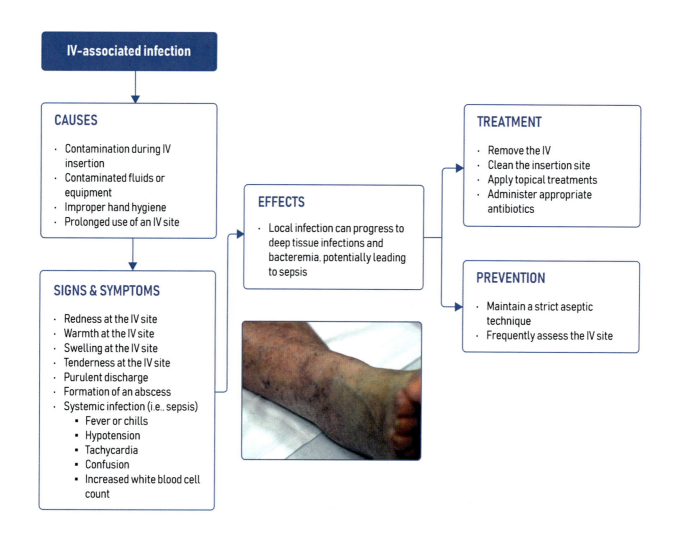

8.6 Intra-arterial injection

Intra-arterial injection, a less common but potentially serious complication of IV medication administration, occurs when a substance intended for venous delivery is mistakenly injected into an artery. Intra-arterial injections can lead to severe local and systemic effects, depending on the type of substance injected, the amount, and the location of the arterial system affected. The high-pressure environment of arteries, combined with the differing chemical properties of medications intended for venous use, can result in immediate damage to arterial walls, reduced blood flow, and ischemia of the tissues served by the affected artery.

Causes: Accidental insertion of an IV cannula into an artery instead of a vein due to a mistake, inadequate lighting or visibility, or the lack of anatomical knowledge.

Signs & symptoms: Bright red blood in the flashback chamber, severe pain at the injection site radiating along the limb, marked pallor, cool skin, cyanosis, prolonged capillary refill time, and weak or absent pulses distal to the injection site.

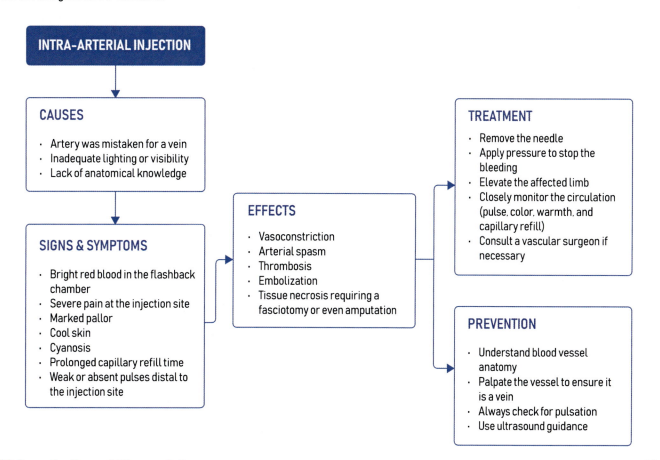

Fig-8-139. Arterial lines look very similar to IV infusion catheters. However, as opposed to an IV injection, intra-arterial injection of medications can result in complications, including ischemia of the extremities and gangrene of fingers. Therefore, the arterial line catheters must be clearly labeled as "ARTERIAL CATHETER" to avoid injection errors.

Effects: Vasoconstriction, arterial spasm, thrombosis, and embolization, leading to compromised blood flow and potential ischemia, resulting in tissue necrosis requiring a fasciotomy or even amputation.

Treatment: Remove the needle and apply pressure to stop the bleeding. Elevate the affected limb and closely monitor the circulation (pulse, color, warmth, and capillary refill). Consult a vascular surgeon if necessary.

Prevention: Understand the anatomy of the blood vessels palpate the vessel to ensure it is a vein, always check for pulsation, and use ultrasound guidance if available.

INTRA-ARTERIAL INJECTION

CAUSES
- Artery was mistaken for a vein
- Inadequate lighting or visibility
- Lack of anatomical knowledge

SIGNS & SYMPTOMS
- Bright red blood in the flashback chamber
- Severe pain at the injection site
- Marked pallor
- Cool skin
- Cyanosis
- Prolonged capillary refill time
- Weak or absent pulses distal to the injection site

EFFECTS
- Vasoconstriction
- Arterial spasm
- Thrombosis
- Embolization
- Tissue necrosis requiring a fasciotomy or even amputation

TREATMENT
- Remove the needle
- Apply pressure to stop the bleeding
- Elevate the affected limb
- Closely monitor the circulation (pulse, color, warmth, and capillary refill)
- Consult a vascular surgeon if necessary

PREVENTION
- Understand blood vessel anatomy
- Palpate the vessel to ensure it is a vein
- Always check for pulsation
- Use ultrasound guidance

8.7 Air embolism

Air embolism, a potentially life-threatening condition, can occur during IV catheterization and therapy when air enters the circulatory system. An air embolism happens when air bubbles enter a vein or artery and travel through the bloodstream to block blood vessels. Although small amounts of air often dissolve in the blood harmlessly, larger volumes can obstruct vascular flow, leading to organ dysfunction and potentially fatal outcomes. In the context of IV therapy, air embolism is a rare but serious complication.

Causes: An air embolism can occur if air enters the circulatory system due to a break in the system, improper equipment connection allowing air to enter, failure to remove air from a syringe or IV tubing, or the insertion or removal of central lines without adequate precautions.

Signs & symptoms:

- **Venous air embolism:** Sudden respiratory distress, hypoxia, hypotension, cyanosis, tachycardia, chest pain, confusion, loss of consciousness, and possibly a "mill-wheel" murmur heard through a stethoscope placed on the chest.
- **Arterial air embolism:** Stroke-like symptoms, such as difficulty speaking, visual disturbances, paralysis, or weakness on one side of the body.

Effects: An air embolism blocks the blood flow to vital organs, causing myocardial infarction, stroke, organ failure, and potentially death.

Treatment: Place the patient in the left lateral decubitus position (Durant's maneuver) to trap air in the right atrium and prevent it from traveling to the lungs. Administer 100% oxygen to increase the resorption of air. Supportive treatments may be necessary, including IV fluids, vasopressors, and respiratory support. Consider hyperbaric oxygen therapy if severe. Start with cardiopulmonary resuscitation if necessary.

Prevention: Prime the IV line. Regularly inspect and maintain the IV infusion. Monitor patients continuously to detect complications early. Remove central lines with the patient in the Trendelenburg position and instruct them to perform the Valsalva maneuver during the removal to prevent air entry under negative pressure that can occur during breathing.

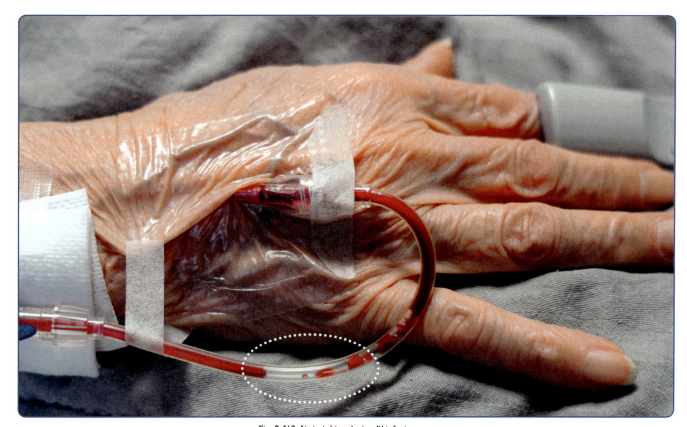

Fig-8-140. Air in tubing during IV infusion.

AIR EMBOLISM

CAUSES
- Failure to remove air from the syringe or IV tubing
- Disconnected IV tubing
- Infusion pump malfunction
- Insertion or removal of central lines without adequate precautions

SIGNS & SYMPTOMS
- Venous air embolism
  - Respiratory distress
  - Hypoxia
  - Cyanosis
  - Tachycardia
  - Chest pain
  - Mill-wheel murmur
  - Confusion
  - Loss of consciousness
- Arterial air embolism
  - Difficulty speaking
  - Visual disturbances
  - Paralysis
  - Weakness on one side

EFFECTS
- Blocks blood flow to vital organs
  - Heart attack
  - Stroke
  - Organ failure
  - Respiratory distress
  - Death

TREATMENT
- Place the patient in the left lateral decubitus position
- Administer 100% oxygen
- Consider supportive treatments
  - IV fluids
  - Vasopressors
  - Respiratory support
- Consider hyperbaric oxygen therapy if severe
- Start with cardiopulmonary resuscitation if necessary

PREVENTION
- Prime the IV line
- Always use the correct technique for IV insertion
- Regularly inspect and maintain the IV equipment
- Monitor patients continuously to detect any issues early
- When removing a central line
  - Place the patient in the Trendelenburg position
  - Instruct the patient to perform the Valsalva maneuver

09

Scan the QR code for IV technique videos

ULTRASOUND-GUIDED PERIPHERAL VENOUS ACCESS

Ultrasound-guided peripheral venous cannulation uses real-time (dynamic) ultrasound to guide venipuncture and peripheral IV catheter placement usually into a deep, nonpalpable upper arm vein. Ultrasound guidance can be a game-changer when equipped with the right tools and skilled professionals.

9.1 Indications for ultrasound-guided peripheral IV cannulation

In IV therapy, ultrasound-guided peripheral IV cannulation has emerged as an important technique, enhancing the success rates of venous access, especially in patients with difficult venous anatomy. Ultrasound guidance for peripheral IV cannulation represents a significant advancement in venous access. It provides real-time visualization of veins, surrounding tissues, and the needle path. It is particularly beneficial for patients with difficult access due to obesity, chronic illness, or depleted venous reserves. This technique enhances the accuracy of needle insertion, minimizes the number of attempts required for successful cannulation, and increases patient comfort and satisfaction.

Ultrasound guidance is commonly used for peripheral IV cannulation in these scenarios:

- **Difficult venous access:** Patients with multiple failed IV attempts by traditional methods or those with a known history of difficult access.
- **Obesity:** Increased subcutaneous fat can make traditional landmark-based methods challenging.
- **Chronic illness or therapy:** Patients with chronic diseases like end-stage renal disease or those on chemotherapy often have exhausted peripheral veins.
- **Pediatric patients:** Their smaller vein size can make traditional IV cannulations challenging.
- **Elderly patients:** Aging skin and veins can make traditional IV placement more difficult.
- **Burn victims:** Burned skin or tissue may obscure or damage veins, making the ultrasound technique a safer and more effective alternative.
- **Edematous skin:** Fluid accumulation in the extremities can obscure veins.
- **History of IV drug abuse:** These patients often have damaged or sclerosed veins.
- **Severe dehydration:** Dehydration can lead to decreased blood volume, causing peripheral veins to collapse and become less palpable and visible to the naked eye.
- **Hypercoagulable states:** Patients at high risk for DVT might benefit from visualization of the deep veins during peripheral IV cannulation.

We emphasize to the reader that while this manual primarily concentrates on traditional techniques for IV access, this section is included for completeness. Ultrasound-guided IV access is becoming increasingly prevalent for difficult IV situations. For a more comprehensive understanding and detailed information on ultrasound-guided IV access, readers are encouraged to consult additional resources provided by NYSORA and other authorities elsewhere.

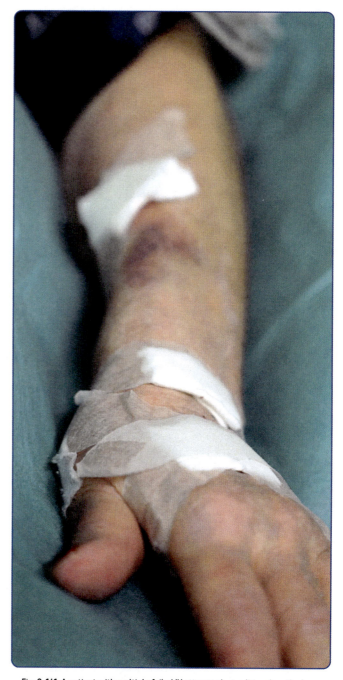

Fig-9-141. A patient with multiple failed IV attempts by traditional methods can benefit from ultrasound-guided cannulation.

9.2 Transducer-needle orientation

Two views are typically used in ultrasound-guided peripheral venous cannulation: in-plane and out-of-plane. The orientation of the needle with respect to the ultrasound transducer determines whether the needle is in-plane or out-of-plane.

In-plane

- **Description:** In-plane is a long-axis approach of the needle. The transducer is aligned with the plane. This view is technically more difficult to obtain as the transducer, vein, and needle all need to be kept in one plane.
- **Visualization:** The entire needle length can be seen as a straight line on the ultrasound screen.
- **Advantages:** The entire shaft of the needle can be visualized, reducing the risk of complications due to unintended needle advancement.
- **Disadvantages:** Requires more space to maneuver as the needle and transducer are aligned in the same plane.

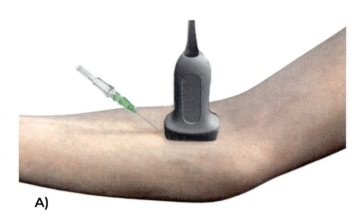

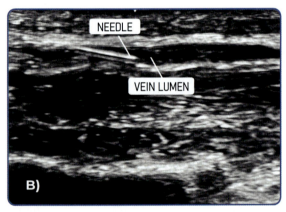
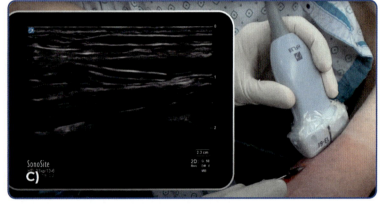

Fig-9-142. A) Illustration of in-plane needle insertion. B) Ultrasound image of in-plane needle insertion. C) In-plane visualization of the needle using ultrasound guidance.

Out-of-plane

- **Description:** The out-of-plane technique positions the transducer in a transverse or short-axis orientation with respect to the needle.
- **Visualization:** Only a small cross-section of the needle can be seen on the ultrasound screen, typically as a hyperechoic (white) small dot or circle.
- **Advantages:** This approach requires less space for needle insertion and can be advantageous in anatomically challenging areas.
- **Disadvantages:** It is harder to determine the exact depth and position as the needle tip can be distinguished only by the appearance and disappearance of the white dot as the imaging plane traverses the needle tip.
- **Note:** The out-of-plane view is usually preferred for vascular access because it is easy to obtain and is the best for identifying veins and arteries and their orientation relative to each other.

> Access the videos for this section by scanning the QR code at the beginning of the chapter.

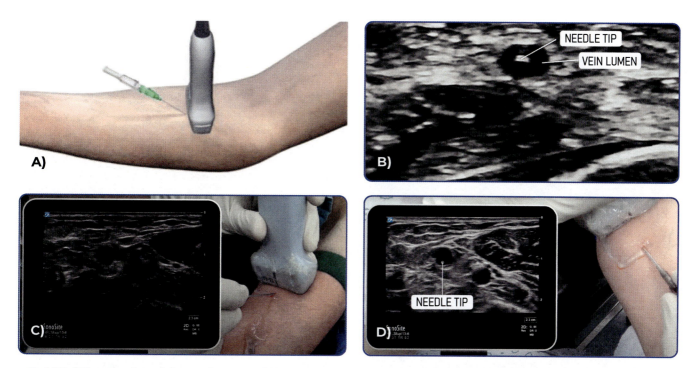

Fig-9-143. A) Illustration of out-of-plane needle insertion. B) Ultrasound image of out-of-plane needle insertion. C) Out-of-plane visualization of the needle using ultrasound guidance. D) Out-of-plane visualization of the needle tip using ultrasound guidance.

> **TIPS**
> - Align the transducer marker with the screen marker for clarity.
> - Apply enough gel and place the transducer directly on the skin to get a clear image.
> - Do not apply too much pressure on the ultrasound transducer to avoid vein collapse.
> - If there is difficulty in visualizing the needle tip, adjust the transducer's position rather than the needle.

9.3 Technique

Patient preparation

- Common targets for ultrasound-guided IV placement include the deep forearm veins and the brachial vein.
- Place the patient comfortably with the target area exposed.
- Adjust the bed height to avoid bending over during the procedure.
- Rest the body part being cannulated on a comfortable surface and adjust the position to expose the site optimally. To cannulate the brachial or the basilic vein, abduct and externally rotate the arm to expose the medial upper arm.
- Apply the tourniquet.
- Disinfect the insertion site.

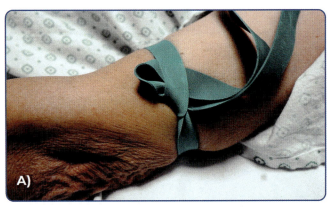 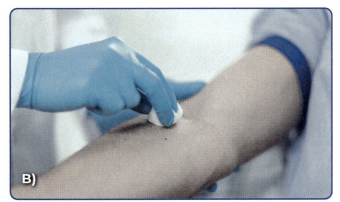

Fig-9-144. A) Tourniquet application. B) Disinfection of the insertion area.

Ultrasound setup

- Use a probe cover.
- Set the machine to 2D mode.
- Choose the appropriate setting (usually labeled vascular or similar).
- Set the maximum depth at the surface of a bone to view the entire field.

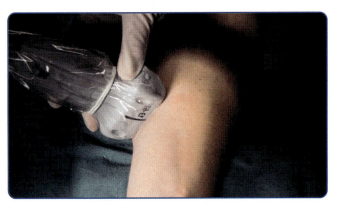 

Fig-9-145. Always use sterile probe covers during ultrasound-guided IV access to prevent cross-patient and equipment contamination.

Scan the vein

- Start with the transducer in a transverse or out-of-plane orientation to visualize the vein in cross-section.
- Perform a preliminary non-sterile ultrasound inspection to identify a suitable vein; a preferred vein segment is straight, wide, relatively close to the surface, and distinct from a nearby artery.
- Identify the vein as a dark, compressible, non-pulsatile structure and understand in which way the vein travels.
- If needed, switch to a longitudinal or in-plane view to visualize the length of the vein.

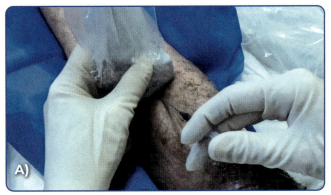 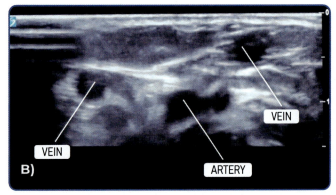

Fig-9-146. A) Start with the transducer in a transverse or out-of-plane orientation. B) Visualize the artery and veins in the forearm.

Pre-insertion considerations

- Confirm that it is a vein and not an artery.

	Artery	Vein
Pulsatile	Yes	No
Compressible	Resistant	Yes
Respiratory variation	No	Yes
Valves	No	Yes
Wall	Thick	Thin
Color Doppler	Distal flow direction	Proximal flow direction
Pulsed wave Doppler	High speed directed distally	Low speed directed proximally

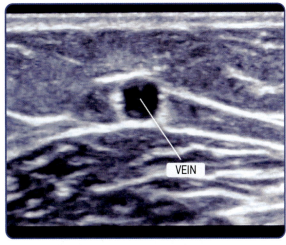

Fig-9-147. Vein of interest shown on ultrasound.

- Verify if the vein's size and depth are suitable for cannulation.
- Check for any nearby structures, such as arteries or nerves.

> **TIP**
> When using color Doppler for ultrasound-guided IV catheterization, it's essential not to use a tourniquet. The use of a tourniquet can hinder venous blood flow, which may adversely affect the visualization of veins using Doppler imaging.

Needle insertion

- Hold the transducer steady with one hand while using the other for the needle.
- Insert the needle out-of-plane with the bevel facing up at an angle that matches the vein's direction.
- Insert the needle about 5 mm into the skin to visualize the needle.
- If the needle is inserted too superficially, the ultrasound might not clearly show the needle tip.

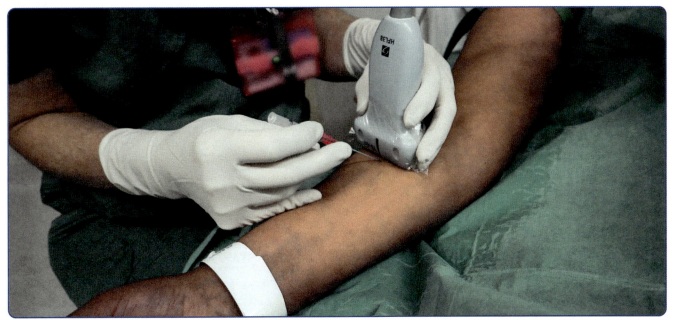

Fig-9-148. Out-of-plane needle insertion using ultrasound guidance.

09 Ultrasound-guided peripheral venous access

- Use the **"creep up technique"** to track the needle tip continuously on ultrasound while advancing the needle:
  - Slowly move the needle and the transducer together when the needle tip enters the vein on the ultrasound screen.
  - As the needle is pushed deeper into the vein, slide the transducer slightly in the same direction.
  - This helps to keep track of the needle tip in the vein.

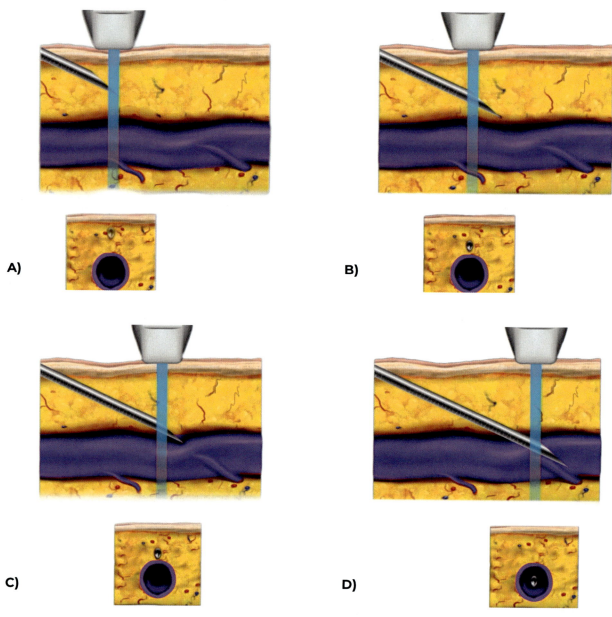

Fig-9-149. Use the "creep up technique" to track the needle tip continuously on ultrasound while advancing the needle.

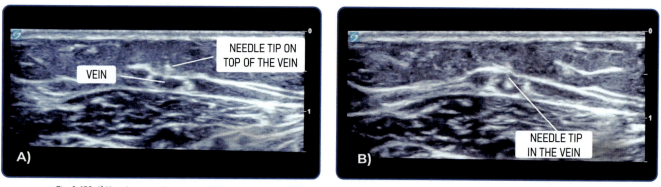

Fig-9-150. A) Visualization of the needle tip on top of the vein with ultrasound. B) Confirmation of needle placement in the vein with ultrasound.

> **TIPS**
> - It's essential not to focus solely on your hands. A common error for beginners is to rely only on the feel of their hands and look away from the ultrasound screen or the other way around.
> - Keep switching attention from the screen to the site of needle insertion to ensure that the needle and ultrasound transducer are continuously aligned.
> - Always maintain ultrasound visualization of the needle tip during insertion.
> - Be aware that a needle can appear within the lumen of the vein without actually puncturing the vein's wall.

Catheter advancement

- Continue to advance the needle within the vein under ultrasound guidance until the needle is seen inside the vein. Usually, the entrance of the needle into the vein is associated with a certain "pop" feeling and the appearance of blood in the flashback chamber.
- Verify the correct placement of the IV by using a longitudinal or in-plane view.
- Thread the catheter off the needle into the vein.
- Retract the needle while leaving the catheter inside the vein.
- Attach the IV tubing, aspirate to confirm catheter placement, and flush the catheter.

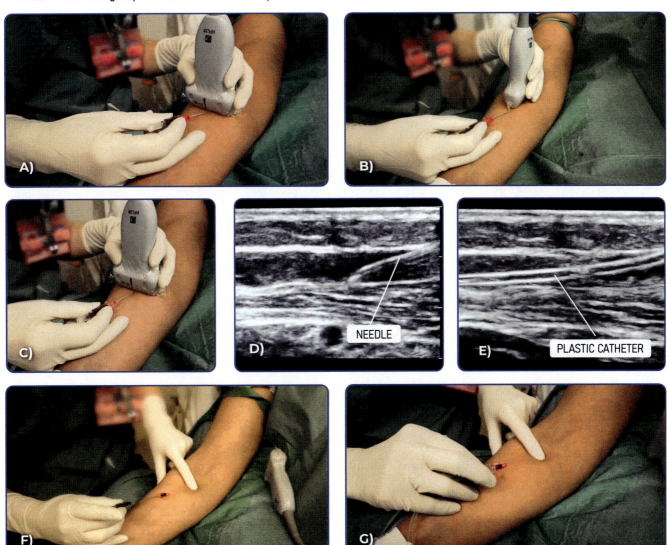

Fig-9-151. A) Observation of blood flashback. B) Verify the correct placement of the IV with a longitudinal or in-plane view. C) Lower the angle to advance the needle. D) Longitudinal ultrasound view of the needle in the vein. E) Visualization of the plastic catheter advancing in the vein with ultrasound. F) Put the index finger over the insertion site to avoid blood leakage and retract the needle. G) Attach the IV tubing.

Securement

- Secure the IV line with adhesive strips, a securement device, and/or a sterile dressing to stabilize the catheter.

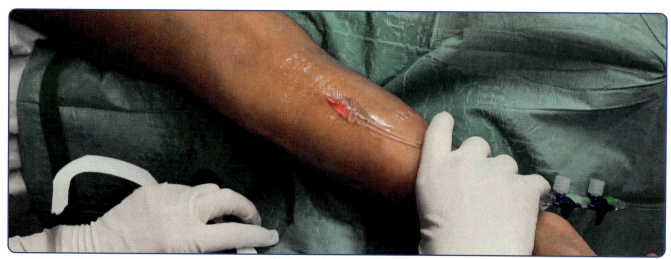

Fig-9-152. Secure the IV line with a sterile dressing.

> **TIPS**
> - Maintain a steady hand by resting it on the patient's skin, which helps accommodate any slight patient movements.
> - Awareness is key to prevent inadvertent hand movement that may occur when the focus shifts from the screen to the needle.

> Access the videos for this section by scanning the QR code at the beginning of the chapter.

9.4 Tips

- Ultrasound-guided IV access is often easier using the out-of-plane technique.
- A linear transducer is most commonly used.
- IV cannulation with ultrasound guidance has fewer complications. However, take caution to avoid accidental arterial punctures.
- For confirming vein location:
    - Veins compress easily with light pressure from the ultrasound transducer.
    - Veins do not exhibit a pulse.
    - Use color Doppler if available to distuingish veins from arteries.
- Remember, ultrasound-guided IV cannulation often needs a longer catheter. This is due to the vein's deeper location and the sharper approach angle.
- Patient comfort and reassurance are vital. Many patients requiring ultrasound guidance have experienced previous failed IV attempts, leading to potential frustration. Ensure that patients feel informed and supported. Use local anesthetic infiltration (1% lidocaine) before ultrasound-guided IV cannulation, which often takes a longer time than the traditional technique without ultrasound.

9.5 Algorithm

Ultrasound-guided IV cannulation

PATIENT PREPARATION
- Comfortable position with the target area exposed
- Brachial or basilic vein: Abduct and externally rotate the arm to expose the medial upper arm
- Apply a tourniquet

ULTRASOUND SETUP
- Linear transducer
- 2D mode (vascular setting optional)
- Adjust the depth and gain (as required)
- Increase the gain setting
- Consider using the zoom function

SCAN THE VEIN
- Start with the transducer in the transverse or out-of-plane orientation
- Perform a preliminary non-sterile ultrasound inspection to identify a suitable vein
- Identify the vein as a dark, compressible, non-pulsatile structure
- If needed, switch to a longitudinal or in-plane view to visualize the length of the vein

PRE-INSERTION CONSIDERATIONS
- Use a sterile probe cover
- Confirm that it is a vein and not an artery (can use Doppler)
- Verify that the vein's size and depth are suitable for cannulation
- Check for any nearby structures, such as arteries or nerves
- Disinfect the extremity

NEEDLE INSERTION
- Insert the needle out-of-plane with the bevel facing up at an angle that matches the vein direction
- Use the "creep up technique" to track the needle tip
- Always maintain ultrasound visualization of the needle tip during insertion

CATHETER ADVANCEMENT
- Thread the catheter off the needle and into the vein
- Continue to advance the catheter until blood is seen in the flashback chamber
- Retract the needle while leaving the catheter inside the vein
- Attach the IV tubing
- Aspirate to confirm catheter placement
- Flush the catheter

SECUREMENT
- Secure the IV line
- Verify the correct placement of the IV by using a longitudinal or in-plane view

Fig-9-153. Always use sterile probe covers during ultrasound-guided IV access to prevent cross-patient, and equipment contamination.

10

Scan the QR code for IV technique videos

IV CATHETERIZATION IN THE CENTRAL VENOUS SYSTEM

Central venous access involves inserting a central venous catheter (CVC) in a larger vein, such as the **external or internal jugular**, **subclavian**, or **femoral vein.**
CVCs offer a direct route to the heart and central circulation, facilitating the administration of medications, fluids, nutritional support, and monitoring central venous pressure. They are indispensable when peripheral venous access is inadequate or when the patient requires long-term IV therapy or frequent blood sampling.

Given the complexity and potential risks associated with central venous access, including infection, thrombosis, and mechanical complications, this chapter emphasizes the importance of understanding the anatomy, selecting the appropriate type of catheter, and mastering the insertion technique.

Indications	Complications
· Long-term IV treatment for antibiotics, chemotherapy, or nutrition · Difficult peripheral venous access · Limited access elsewhere · Central venous pressure monitoring · Rapid fluid replacement · Large-bore access · Administration of high-risk medications such as vasopressors (cause harm if leaked into the tissues) · Hemodialysis or plasmapheresis	· Pneumothorax · Arterial puncture · Hematoma · Hemothorax · Air embolism · Arrhythmias · Infection · Sepsis · Thrombosis · Catheter misplacement in the internal jugular vein or thoracic duct

10.1 Types of central venous catheters

Numerous varieties of central venous catheters exist, each distinguished by unique features, benefits, and limitations. The best catheter for each indication is chosen based on the patient's vein size and the type of fluid or medication to be administered.

Peripherally inserted central catheter (PICC)

A central catheter is inserted in a peripheral vein. These are safer than central venous catheters as risks such as a collapsed lung or blood in the chest cavity are avoided.
- **Location:** Inserted through a peripheral vein (i.e., basilic, brachial, or cephalic vein) and navigated into a central vein close to the heart.
- **Use:** Prolonged IV antibiotic therapy, chemotherapy, or long-term total parenteral nutrition.
- **Characteristics:** PICCs have a long length, and their tip lies close to the heart.

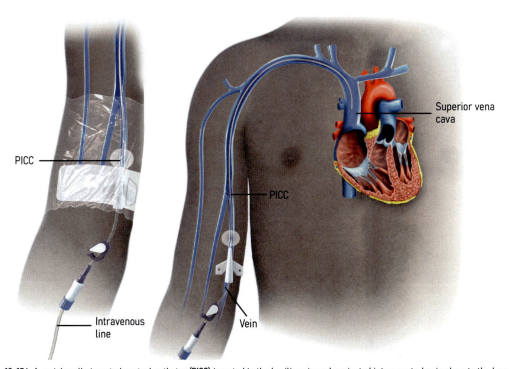

Fig-10-154. A peripherally inserted central catheter (PICC) inserted in the basilic vein and navigated into a central vein close to the heart.

Central venous catheter (CVC)

- **Description:** Unlike PICCs, CVCs are inserted directly into a central vein, such as the subclavian vein, jugular vein, or femoral vein. This provides immediate central venous access for the administration of medications, fluids, and for critical monitoring purposes.
- **Use:** CVCs are often required in critical care, surgical settings, or in situations where rapid and direct access to the central venous system is necessary. They are essential for hemodynamic monitoring, emergency resuscitation, and administering medications that are too irritative for peripheral veins.
- **Characteristics:** CVCs are shorter than PICCs because they do not need to be threaded through peripheral veins. Their central placement allows for accurate monitoring of central venous pressure and other critical care interventions.
- **Risks:** The insertion of CVCs carries a higher risk of immediate complications, such as pneumothorax or hemothorax, due to the proximity of the insertion sites to the lungs and major blood vessels. The risk of infection and thrombosis remains a concern, as with any central venous access device, necessitating strict adherence to aseptic technique during insertion and meticulous care throughout the catheter's use.

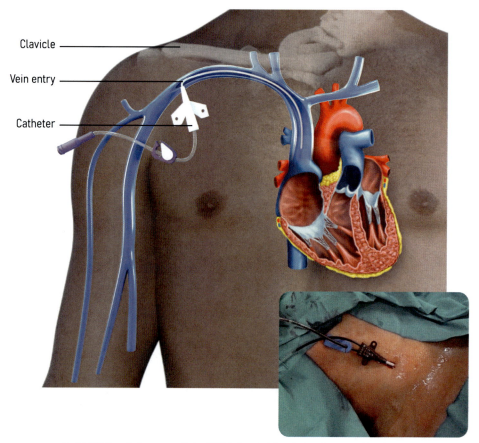

Fig-10-155. A central venous catheter (CVC) is inserted directly into the internal jugular vein.

Tunneled catheter

- **Description:** Tunneled catheters are inserted into a central vein, but unlike non-tunneled catheters, a portion of the catheter is tunneled under the skin for several centimeters from the insertion site before it enters the vein. This tunnel acts as a barrier to pathogens, reducing the risk of infection.
- **Use:** They are typically used for long-term IV therapy, such as chemotherapy, long-term antibiotic therapy, or total parenteral nutrition. The tunneling process also helps to secure the catheter in place, reducing the risk of accidental dislodgement.
- **Advantages:** The primary advantage of tunneled catheters is their lower infection rate compared to non-tunneled catheters, due to the barrier created by the tunnel. They also tend to be more comfortable for long-term use and allow patients more mobility than non-tunneled catheters.

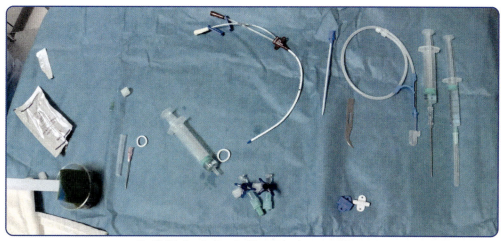

Fig-10-156. Supplies required for a central venous catheter.

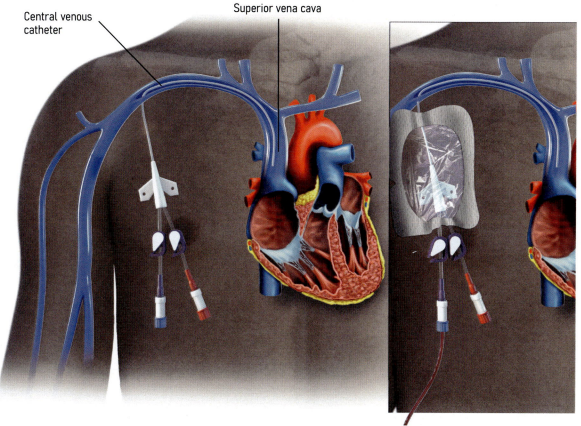

Fig-10-157. Tunneled catheters are inserted into a central vein.

Non-tunneled catheter

- **Description:** Non-tunneled catheters are directly inserted into a central vein without the creation of a subcutaneous tunnel. They are typically shorter in duration of use compared to tunneled catheters.
- **Use:** These catheters are often used in acute care settings where central venous access is required immediately, for a short duration, such as for emergency resuscitation, acute fluid administration, or during surgeries.
- **Advantages:** The main advantages of non-tunneled catheters include ease and speed of insertion, which is important in emergency situations. However, they carry a higher risk of infection compared to tunneled catheters because the direct path from the skin to the vein offers less resistance to bacterial entry.

10 IV catheterization in the central venous system

Implantable port

- **Description:** An implantable port, or Port-a-cath, consists of a reservoir (the port) that is completely implanted under the skin and a catheter that connects the port to a central vein. Access to the port is gained through the skin with a special needle.
- **Use:** Implantable ports are used for patients who require long-term intermittent access to the venous system for treatments such as chemotherapy, long-term antibiotics, or blood transfusions. They are especially favored in patients leading an active lifestyle or when the aesthetic is a concern.
- **Advantages:** The completely internalized design significantly reduces the risk of infection and allows patients to bathe, swim, and engage in other activities without the risk of dislodging the catheter. Implantable ports require less daily maintenance than external catheters but do require a minor surgical procedure for placement and removal.

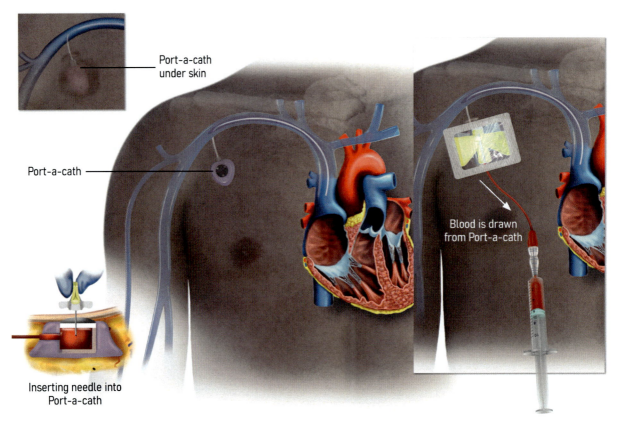

Fig-10-158. An implantable port, or Port-a-cath, consists of a reservoir (the port) that is completely implanted under the skin and a catheter that connects the port to a central vein.

Umbilical catheter

Umbilical catheters are specialized medical devices designed for use in the neonatal population, providing critical access to the circulatory system of newborns through the unique entry point of the umbilical vessels. These catheters utilize the remnants of the umbilical vein and arteries, which remain patent and accessible for a short period after birth, offering a non-invasive method to administer medications, fluids, and for the withdrawal of blood samples, as well as for monitoring blood pressure and obtaining blood gases. Here's a more detailed look at umbilical catheters:

Types of umbilical catheters

- **Umbilical venous catheters:** These are inserted into the umbilical vein and can be used to administer medications, fluids, parenteral nutrition, and to obtain venous access. The umbilical vein offers a direct route to the central circulation, allowing for efficient delivery of substances needed for the care of the neonate.
- **Umbilical artery catheters:** These are placed in one of the umbilical arteries and are primarily used for continuous blood pressure monitoring and frequent blood gas analysis. Umbilical artery catheters provide valuable information on the neonate's oxygenation and perfusion status, which is critical for managing various neonatal conditions.

Advantages

- **Minimally invasive:** Using the umbilical vessels for catheter placement is less invasive than other venous or arterial access methods in neonates, reducing the risk of complications associated with more invasive procedures.
- **Immediate access:** In the immediate postnatal period, the umbilical vessels provide readily accessible routes for establishing vascular access, which is essential for managing critically ill neonates who require immediate interventions.
- **Reduced pain and stress:** Since the umbilical stump is not innervated, the insertion of umbilical catheters causes less pain and stress to the newborn than peripheral or central venous catheterizations.

Considerations and complications

While umbilical catheters are invaluable in neonatal care, their use comes with potential risks and complications, such as infection, thrombosis, and vessel perforation. Therefore, strict aseptic technique during insertion and meticulous care and monitoring during use are essential to minimize these risks. The decision to use an umbilical catheter takes into account the clinical condition of the neonate, the anticipated duration of the need for vascular access, and the potential benefits and risks associated with the procedure.

In summary, umbilical catheters provide a critical, minimally invasive means of vascular access in neonates, facilitating the administration of life-saving treatments and monitoring in the early days of life. Their use, however, requires careful consideration and skilled management to ensure the safety and well-being of the newborn.

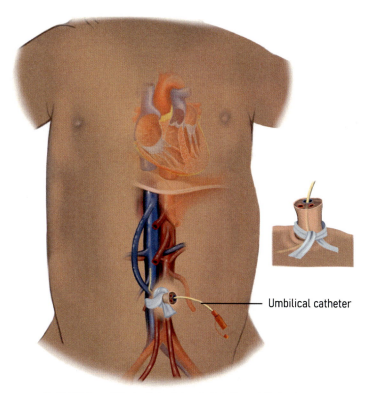

Fig-10-159. An umbilical catheter is inserted into the umbilical vein.

10.2 External or internal jugular vein

Placing an IV into the **external jugular vein (EJV)** or **internal jugular vein (IJV)** is a relatively standard procedure performed in a clinical setting when peripheral venous access is difficult or impossible, in emergencies when other sites are inaccessible, or for short-term central venous access.

External jugular vein (EJV)

The external jugular vein offers a valuable alternative for IV access, especially when traditional peripheral venous access is challenging. The EJV is especially beneficial in emergency settings or for patients with difficult venous access due to factors like obesity, chronic illness, or IV drug use. This approach is often considered when other central lines, such as those in the internal jugular or subclavian veins, are not immediately feasible or are contraindicated. Healthcare professionals, including emergency physicians and nurses, may opt for EJV cannulation to quickly administer fluids and medications or to obtain blood samples when time is of the essence and other access routes are not viable. The decision to use the EJV takes into account the urgency of the situation, the patient's condition, and the clinician's skill and experience with this technique.

> **Access the videos for this section by scanning the QR code at the beginning of the chapter.**

Location and anatomy: The EJV runs superficial and diagonally across the sternocleidomastoid muscle. It is a smaller vein than the IJV.

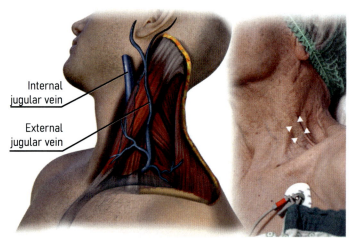

Fig-10-160. Location of the external and internal jugular veins.

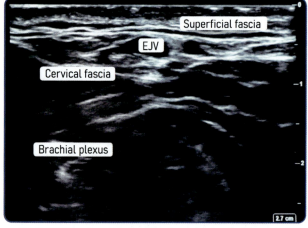

Fig-10-161. The external jugular (EJ) vein can be visualized for central venous access by ultrasound guidance.

EJV cannulation: Commonly used for short-term venous access, such as IV therapy or blood sampling. It's less suitable for long-term use.

Here are the key steps for successful EJV cannulation

Patient position: Place the patient supine with the head slightly extended and turned away from the cannulation site. Elevating the head of the bed about 30 degrees can help to engorge the vein.

Landmark identification: Locate the EJV, which runs diagonally across the sternocleidomastoid muscle. Apply gentle pressure at the base of the neck, above the clavicle, to further engorge the vein, making it more visible and palpable.

Equipment preparation: Prepare all necessary equipment, including an appropriate size cannula, syringe, sterile gauze, and securing materials.

Sterile technique: Maintain an aseptic technique throughout the procedure. Clean the skin over the vein with an appropriate antiseptic solution, and wear sterile gloves.

Local anesthetic application: Use a local anesthetic to numb the area (1-2 mL of 1% lidocaine through a 25-27G needle).

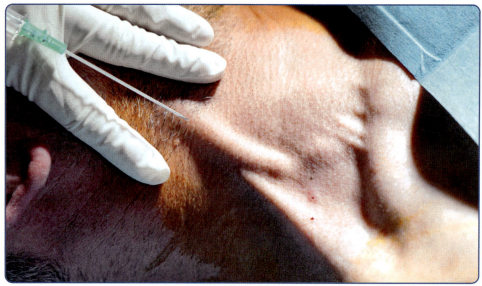

Fig-10-162. Use local anesthetic to numb the external jugular vein cannulation site.

EJV access: EJV access can be accomplished using a needle-catheter system mounted to a 5 mL or 10 mL syringe and advancing at a low angle while aspirating gently for blood return.

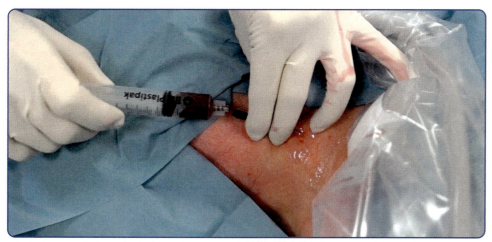

Fig-10-163. Advance the needle-catheter system at a low angle and aspirate for blood return.

The Seldinger technique, as described below, is also commonly used.

1. Puncture the target vein with a thin-walled needle (16G or 18G) connected to a syringe at a 30-45 degree angle to the skin.
2. Use image guidance such as ultrasound for accurate placement.
3. Aspirate frequently and gently until venous blood is aspirated, indicating intravascular needle placement.
4. Insert a guidewire (J-tipped) through the needle into the vein and remove the needle while leaving the guidewire in place.
5. Make a small incision in the skin and insert a dilator to enlarge the opening to insert the CVC (8 French).
6. Thread the CVC over the guidewire into the vein. Ensure the guidewire extends from the IV catheter's end to prevent it from being left inside the patient.
7. Remove the guidewire and dilator while leaving the catheter in place.

TIPS
- Assume a very low angle.
- Place the patient in the Trendelenburg position
- Ask the patient to cough to accentuate the veins.

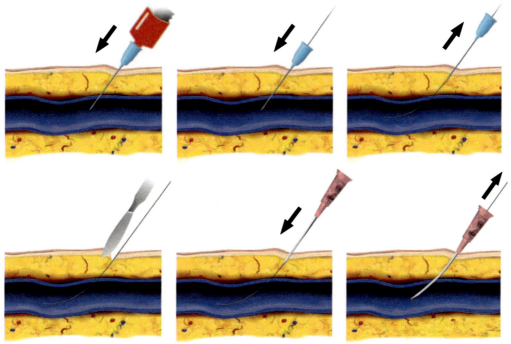

Fig-10-164. Illustration of the Seldinger technique.

Secure the catheter: Secure the cannula with tape once it is correctly positioned. Ensure that it's stable and the patient is comfortable.
Verify placement: Attach a syringe to aspirate blood or connect to an IV line to confirm proper placement and function.
Monitor for complications: Watch for signs such as hematoma, infiltration, or thrombosis during and after the procedure.
Documentation: Record the procedure details, including time, size of the cannula, and any complications or difficulties encountered.

Internal jugular vein (IJV)

Location and anatomy: The IJV is located deep in the sternocleidomastoid muscle. It's a larger vein and lies closer to the central circulation.

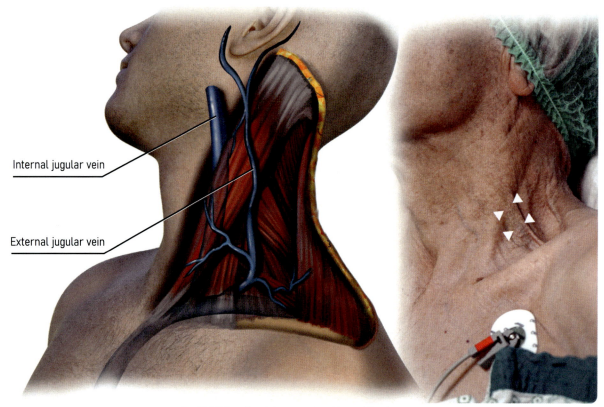

Fig-10-165. Location of the external and internal jugular vein.

IJV cannulation: Often used for central venous pressure monitoring, administering medications or fluids, and hemodialysis. It's preferred for long-term use or in critical care settings.

Here are the key steps for successful IJV cannulation

Patient position: Place the patient supine, with the head slightly tilted back, to enlarge the vein, and turned away from the insertion site.

Landmark identification: The IJV is located deep in the sternocleidomastoid muscle.

Equipment preparation: Prepare all necessary equipment, including an appropriate size cannula, syringe, sterile gauze, and securing materials.

Sterile technique: Maintain an aseptic technique throughout the procedure. Clean the skin over the vein with an appropriate antiseptic solution, and wear sterile gloves.

Local anesthetic application: Use a local anesthetic to numb the area (1-2 mL of 1% lidocaine through a 25-27G needle).

Cannula insertion: Use the **Seldinger technique** to gain IJV access.

1. Puncture the vein with a thin-walled needle (16G or 18G) connected to a syringe at a 30-45 degree angle to the skin. Use image guidance such as ultrasound for accurate placement.
2. Pull back frequently and gently on the syringe plunger until venous blood is aspirated, indicating proper needle placement in the vein.
3. Insert a guidewire (J-tipped) through the needle into the vein and remove the needle while leaving the guidewire in place.
4. Make a small incision in the skin and insert a dilator to enlarge the opening to insert the CVC (8 French).
5. Thread the CVC over the guidewire into the vein. Ensure the guidewire extends from the IV catheter's end to prevent it from being left inside the patient.
6. Remove the guidewire and dilator while leaving the catheter in place.

Secure the cannula: Secure the catheter to the skin using sutures, sterile strips, or an adhesive device, and apply a sterile dressing over the insertion site.

Verify placement: Confirm the position of the catheter with a chest X-ray and check for complications (e.g., pneumothorax).

Monitor for complications: Watch for signs such as hematoma, infiltration, or thrombosis during and after the procedure.

Documentation: Record the procedure details, including time, size of the cannula, and any complications or difficulties encountered.

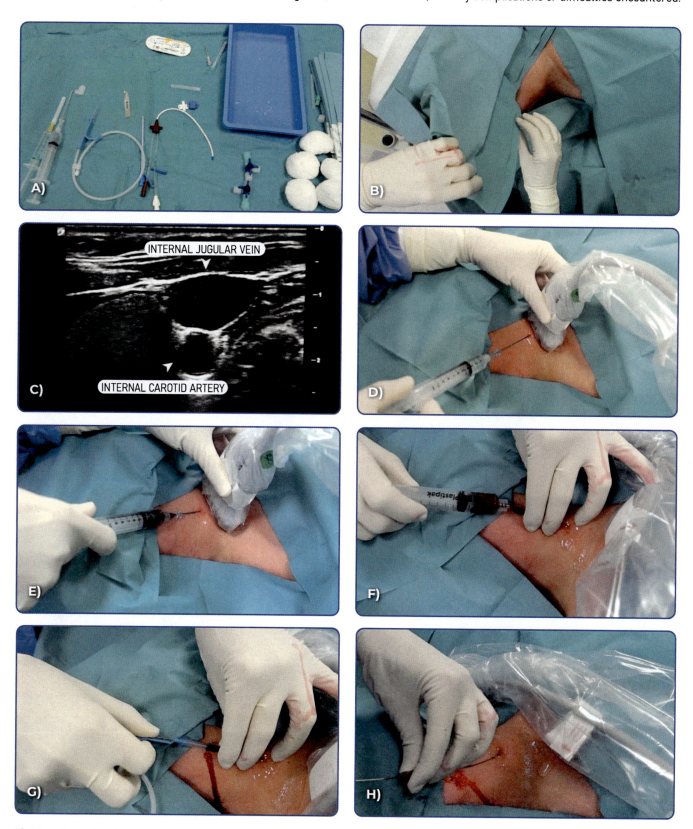

10 IV catheterization in the central venous system

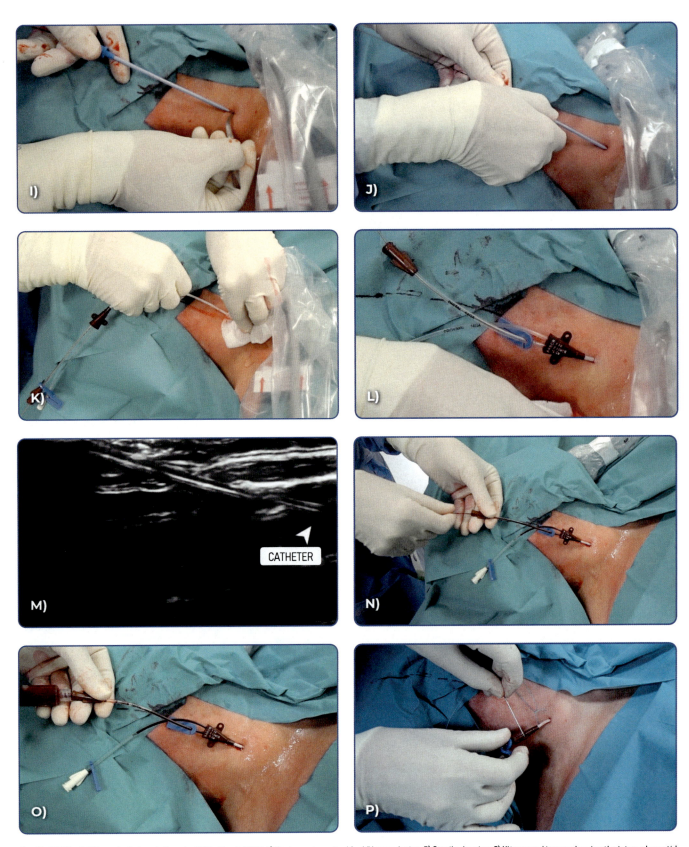

Fig-10-166. The Seldinger technique to insert a CVC in the right IJV. A) Equipment required for IJV cannulation. B) Sterile draping. C) Ultrasound image showing the internal carotid artery and the IJV. D) Puncture of the target vein with a thin-walled needle connected to a syringe using ultrasound guidance. E) Aspiration of venous blood indicates proper needle placement in the vein. F) Disconnection of the syringe. G) Insert a guidewire through the needle into the vein. H) Remove the needle while leaving the guidewire in place. I) Make a small incision in the skin. J) Insert a dilator to enlarge the opening. K) Insert a triple-lumen catheter and ensure the guidewire extends from the IV catheter's end. L) Catheter placement in the IJV. M) Catheter placement confirmed by ultrasound imaging. N) Remove the guidewire while leaving the catheter in place. O) Aspirate and flush the catheter. P) Secure the catheter with sutures.

10.3 Subclavian vein

Subclavian vein cannulation is a another technique for establishing central venous access, offering a direct route for the administration of medications, fluids, parenteral nutrition, and hemodynamic monitoring. This approach may have a lower infection rate compared to other central venous access sites and its usability during cardiopulmonary resuscitation or in patients with severe trauma or burns where peripheral access may be compromised.

The subclavian vein's consistent anatomical location beneath the clavicle provides a relatively stable site for catheter placement, making it a preferred choice in many clinical scenarios, including long-term IV therapy and critical care settings. However, it requires skill and precision due to the proximity to the pleura and major arteries. This emphasizes the importance of expertise and ultrasound guidance to minimize complications such as pneumothorax and arterial puncture.

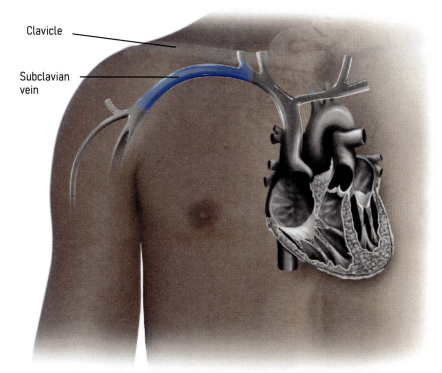

Fig-10-167. Anatomical illustration of the subclavian vein.

Technique using external landmarks

Subclavian vein cannulation using external landmarks, without ultrasound guidance is a challenging procedure and requires precision and expertise.

Patient position: Place the patient supine with a slight Trendelenburg tilt (head lower than feet) to help distend the vein. Use a pillow or towel between the shoulder blades to extend the neck slightly.

Landmark identification: Identify the key landmarks; the sternal and clavicular heads of the sternocleidomastoid muscle, the clavicle, and the suprasternal notch.

Site selection: The subclavian vein is typically accessed just below the junction of the middle and medial third of the clavicle.

Equipment preparation: Assemble all necessary equipment, including a cannulation kit, sterile gloves, drapes, antiseptic solution, and local anesthetic.

Sterile technique: Maintain a strict aseptic technique throughout the procedure. Clean the skin thoroughly with an antiseptic solution and drape the area to maintain a sterile field.

Local anesthetic: Use a local anesthetic to numb the puncture site (2-3 mL of 1% lidocaine).

Needle insertion: Hold the needle between the thumb and index finger, with the bevel facing upward. Insert the needle inferior to the clavicle, directing it slightly laterally and posteriorly toward the suprasternal notch.

Aspirate while advancing: Gently aspirate while slowly advancing the needle. The subclavian vein lies 2 to 4 cm beneath the skin in most patients.

Watch for blood return: Blood return in the syringe indicates successful cannulation. At this point, decrease the insertion angle and advance the guidewire through the needle.

Catheter placement: Once the guidewire is in place, remove the needle and thread the catheter over the guidewire.

Secure the cannula: Secure the catheter to the skin using sutures, sterile strips, or an adhesive device. Apply a sterile dressing over the insertion site.

Verify placement: Confirm the catheter's position either through aspiration of venous blood or by observing the appropriate waveform on a pressure transducer, if available.

Post-procedure care: Monitor the puncture site for signs of infection or hematoma. Watch for any symptoms suggestive of complications, such as pneumothorax or hemothorax.

Documentation: Record the procedure details, including the size of the needle and catheter, the number of attempts, and any complications.

Due to this procedure's complexity and potential risks, it should only be performed by healthcare professionals with specific training and expertise in subclavian vein cannulation or under strict supervision by an experienced clinician.

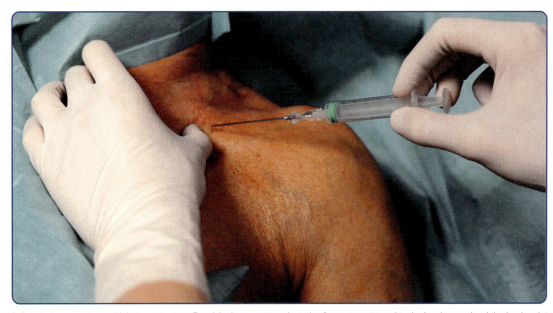

Fig-10-168. Subclavian cannulation: With the patient in a Trendelenburg position, the index finger is positioned in the jugular notch, while the thumb is slightly pushing underneath the clavicle. The needle is inserted in the direction of the thumb to the index finger, underneath the clavicle, to access the subclavian vein.

Ultrasound-Guided Technique

Ultrasound-guided subclavian vein cannulation is a procedure that enhances safety and accuracy by using ultrasound imaging.

Patient position: Place the patient supine with a slight Trendelenburg tilt (head lower than feet) to help distend the vein. Use a pillow or towel between the shoulder blades to extend the neck slightly.

Ultrasound machine setup: Ensure the ultrasound machine is set up with a high-frequency linear transducer, which is ideal for vascular access.

Optimal vein visualization: Adjust the transducer orientation to get the best longitudinal or transverse view of the subclavian vein. The transverse view is often preferred for real-time needle guidance.

Scanning and landmark identification: Scan the area to identify the subclavian vein and artery. The vein is typically compressible and appears anechoic (dark) on ultrasound. Familiarize yourself with the anatomical landmarks and the relationship between the vein and artery.

Site selection: The subclavian vein is typically accessed just below the junction of the middle and medial third of the clavicle.

Equipment preparation: Assemble all necessary equipment, including a cannulation kit, sterile gloves, drapes, antiseptic solution, and local anesthetic.

Sterile technique: Maintain a strict aseptic technique throughout the procedure. Clean the skin thoroughly with an antiseptic solution and drape the area to maintain a sterile field. Use a sterile probe cover and sterile gel.

Local anesthetic: If necessary, inject a local anesthetic under ultrasound guidance to numb both the skin and the path intended for venous puncture.

Needle insertion: Insert the needle under real-time ultrasound guidance. Always visualize the needle tip to ensure accurate placement and to avoid accidental arterial puncture or other complications.

Aspirate while advancing: Gently aspirate while slowly advancing the needle. The subclavian vein lies 2 to 4 cm beneath the skin in most patients.

Watch for blood return: Blood in the flashback chamber indicates successful cannulation. At this point, decrease the insertion angle and advance the guidewire through the needle.

Catheter placement: After successful guidewire insertion, thread the catheter over the guidewire and remove the guidewire.

Verify placement: Confirm the catheter's placement within the vein using ultrasound. This step is important to ensure correct positioning and rule out misplacement or complications like arterial puncture.

Secure the cannula: Secure the catheter to the skin using sutures, sterile strips, or an adhesive device. Apply a sterile dressing over the insertion site.

Post-procedure care: Monitor the puncture site for signs of infection or hematoma. Watch for any symptoms suggestive of complications, such as pneumothorax or hemothorax.

Documentation: Record the procedure details, including the size of the needle and catheter, number of attempts, ultrasound findings, and any complications.

Ultrasound-guided subclavian vein cannulation requires skill and practice. It should be performed by healthcare professionals trained in ultrasound-guided vascular access techniques.

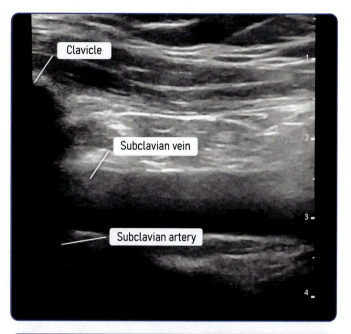

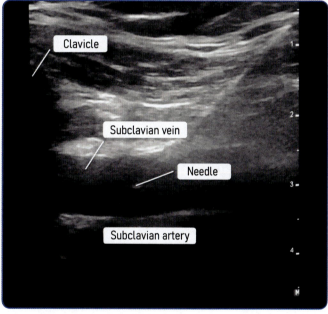

Fig-10-169. Subclavian vein cannulation with ultrasound guidance.

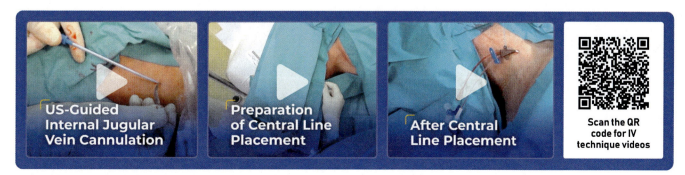

10 IV catheterization in the central venous system

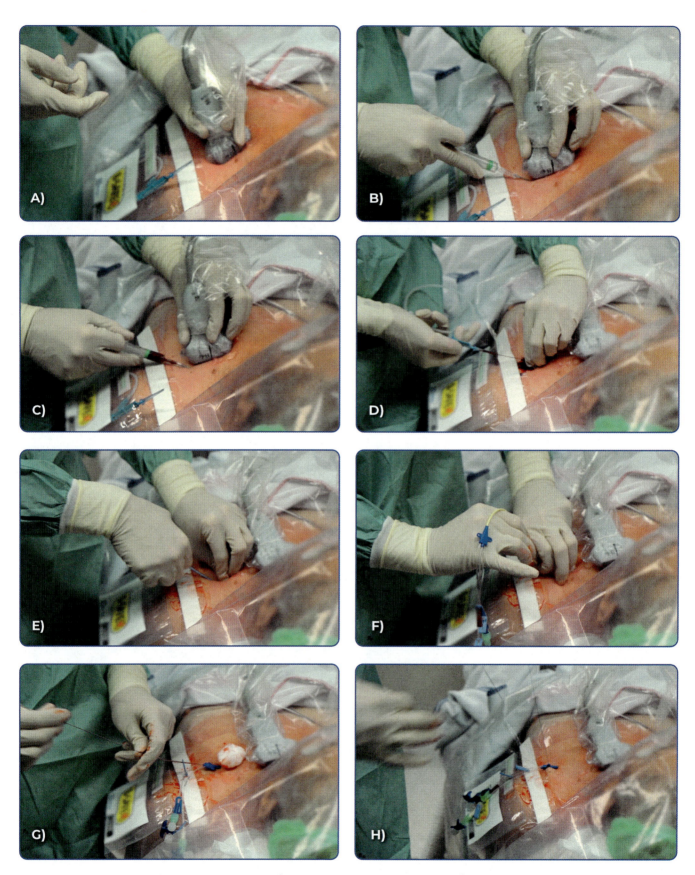

Fig-10-170. Ultrasound-guided cannulation of the subclavian vein. A) Ultrasound scanning of the subclavian vein. B) Puncture of the target vein with a thin-walled needle connected to a syringe using ultrasound guidance. C) Aspiration of venous blood indicates proper needle placement in the vein. D) Insert a guidewire through the needle into the vein. E) Insert a dilator to enlarge the opening. F) Insert a triple-lumen catheter over the guidewire in the subclavian vein and ensure the guidewire extends from the IV catheter's end. G) Remove the guidewire while leaving the catheter in place. H) Secure the catheter with sutures.

10.4 Femoral vein cannulation

Femoral vein cannulation serves as a critical technique for securing central venous access, particularly in emergency situations where traditional access points, such as the subclavian or internal jugular veins, are impractical or inaccessible due to the patient's condition or the situation's urgency.

This method involves inserting a catheter into the femoral vein, located in the groin, to administer medications, and fluids, or for hemodynamic monitoring. While femoral vein access is advantageous for its ease of insertion and accessibility, especially in critically ill patients, it is associated with higher risks of infection and thrombosis. Consequently, femoral vein cannulation is often reserved for short-term use or for patients who are immobilized or on bed rest, where the benefits of quick vascular access outweigh the potential complications.

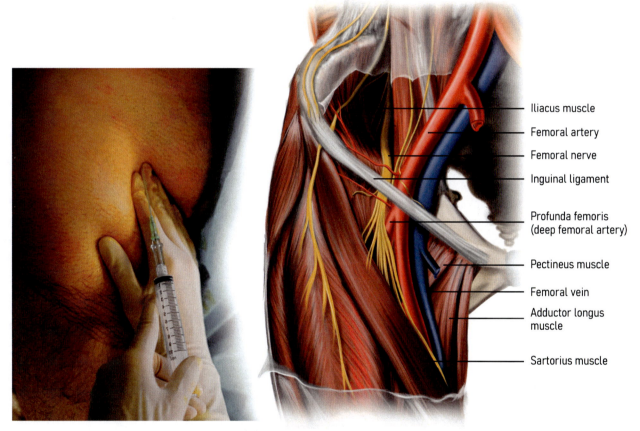

Fig-10-171. Anatomical illustration of the femoral vein.

Here are the key steps for successful femoral vein cannulation

Patient position: Position the patient supine with the legs slightly externally rotated. This position helps to expose the femoral area better.

Landmark identification: First, identify the femoral artery, which pulsates and is located just below the inguinal ligament. The femoral vein is located medial to the femoral artery.

Ultrasound guidance: If available, use ultrasound to locate the femoral vein and guide the cannulation to reduce the risk of complications and improve the success rate.

Equipment preparation: Assemble all necessary equipment, including a cannulation kit, sterile gloves, drapes, antiseptic solution, and local anesthetic.

Sterile technique: Maintain a strict aseptic technique throughout the procedure. Clean the area thoroughly with an antiseptic solution and use sterile drapes, gloves, and equipment.

Local anesthetic: Inject a local anesthetic to numb the skin and deeper tissue at the puncture site.

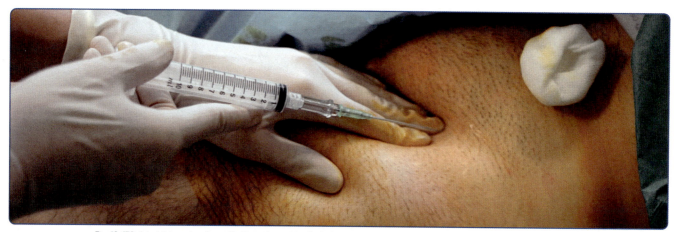

Fig-10-172. Administer a local anesthetic to desensitize both the skin and the underlying tissue at the site of the puncture site.

Needle insertion: Insert the cannulation needle at a 30-45 degree angle, just medial to the femoral artery pulse. Aim the needle slightly cephalad.

Aspirate while advancing: Gently aspirate while slowly advancing the needle. A decrease in resistance and the appearance of venous blood return indicate successful entry into the vein.

Guidewire insertion: Insert the guidewire through the needle after confirming venous access. Ensure smooth advancement without resistance.

Catheter placement: Dilate the tract if necessary, then thread the catheter over the guidewire. Once the catheter is in place, remove the guidewire.

Verify placement: Confirm placement of the catheter tip, ideally using ultrasound. If unavailable, check with an X-ray to ensure correct positioning and rule out complications.

Secure the cannula: Use sutures or an adhesive dressing, as appropriate.

Post-procedure care: Be mindful for potential complications such as hematoma, infection, or accidental arterial puncture.

Documentation: Record the procedure details, including the size of the needle and catheter, the number of attempts, and any complications encountered.

Femoral vein cannulation should be carried out by healthcare professionals who are trained in this procedure and should be assisted by ultrasound guidance to enhance accuracy and minimize the risk of complications.

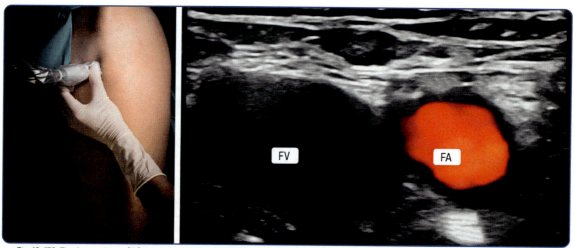

Fig-10-173. The femoral vein (FV) is located medial to the femoral artery (FA) and can be assessed for IV cannulation by ultrasound guidance.

TIPS

- Ultrasound guidance can assist in accurate puncture and reduce complications.
- Replace temporary femoral vein catheters as soon as possible with upper body lines.
- Be aware that during cardiopulmonary arrest, hypotension, or hypoxia, arterial blood might present darker and lack the typical pulsatile flow, making it mistaken for venous blood.

11

Scan the QR code for IV technique videos

IV ACCESS TRAINING AND ASSISTANCE TOOLS

11.1 IV access simulators

Practicing IV cannulation to prevent mistakes from happening is essential, yet gaining experience can be challenging when working directly with patients, as having too many errors in this environment is undesirable. This is where IV simulators become an invaluable tool for medical practitioners. These simulators are designed to closely mimic venous structures, offering a realistic and safe environment for practitioners to develop and refine their cannulation skills.

- **Realistic venous replication:** IV simulators are designed to closely mimic the anatomical structure and feel of veins. This includes variations in vein size, depth, and even elasticity, offering practitioners a realistic experience similar to actual IV cannulation on patients.
- **Safe and risk-free practice:** One of the primary benefits of IV simulators is their safe, risk-free environment. Medical professionals can practice IV insertion techniques without the ethical and medical concerns associated with practicing on actual patients, thus eliminating the risk of patient harm during the learning process. For example, as explained in this manual, new techniques like bending the needle to cannulate difficult superficial veins better might be daunting for the first time in a real-life clinical setting. For these situations, practice on an IV simulator can make a difference in providing skill and confidence to the medical practitioner.
- **Skill development and confidence building:** Regular practice on IV simulators helps clinicians improve their technical skills, hand-eye coordination, and overall confidence in performing IV cannulations. This is especially beneficial for mastering challenging techniques like **ultrasound-guided catheterization.**
- **Feedback and evaluation:** Many advanced IV simulators come equipped with sensors and software that provide immediate feedback to the user. This feedback can include information on the depth and angle of needle insertion, helping learners refine their techniques and learn from their mistakes in real-time.
- **Versatility and customization:** IV simulators come in various models, ranging from basic to advanced, allowing customization of the training experience. They can simulate different patient scenarios, including pediatrics, geriatrics, and patients with varying vein visibility and condition, making them an essential tool for comprehensive IV training across different medical fields.

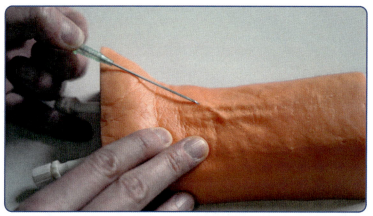

Fig-11-174. Example of an IV access simulator designed to closely mimic venous structures, offering a realistic and safe environment for practitioners to develop and refine their cannulation skills.

Fig-11-175. Medical professionals enhancing their skills with IV simulators.

11.2 Vein finders

Vein finders and illuminators are devices designed to assist healthcare professionals in locating and visualizing veins for IV catheterizations. These devices are particularly useful in patients with difficulties in venous access due obesity, deep skin pigmentation, swelling, dehydration, or in pediatric cases.

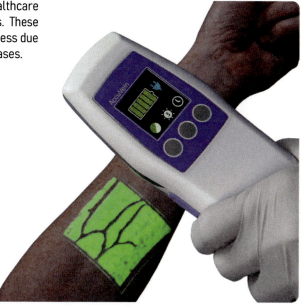

Fig-11-176. AccuVein ® vein finder.

How do they work?

- **Infrared light:** Most vein finders use infrared (IR) light. Veins carry deoxygenated blood, which absorbs infrared light more than the surrounding tissues. When the device emits IR light onto the skin, the veins absorb more of this light, making them appear different from the surrounding tissue.
- **Detection and projection:** The absorbed IR light by the veins is detected by the device's sensors. The device then processes this data, and an image or pattern of the veins is projected directly onto the skin or displayed on a screen.
- **Real-time imaging:** Many modern vein finders offer real-time imaging, allowing practitioners to see any movement or changes in the vein as they work.
- **Adjustable intensities:** Some devices allow users to adjust the intensity of the IR light, which can be helpful for patients with different skin tones or in locations where ambient lighting varies.
- **Portability and usability:** Many vein finders are handheld and battery-operated, making them portable and easy to use in various settings.
- **Enhanced visualization:** Some advanced models provide color differentiation based on the depth and size of the veins.

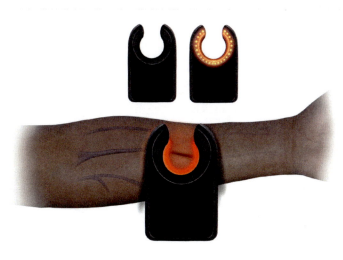

Fig-11-177. Use of a vein illuminator to visualize veins.

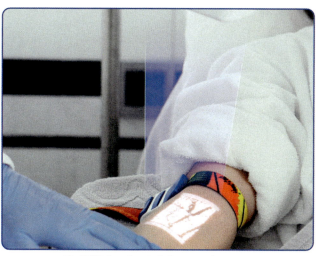

Fig-11-178. Use of a vein finder to visualize veins.

11 IV access training and assistance tools

When to use?

While vein finders can be used for any patient, they are especially beneficial for:
- Pediatric patients, given their smaller and more fragile veins.
- Elderly patients, especially those with delicate veins susceptible to trauma.
- Patients with a history of IV drug use or multiple medical interventions.
- Obese patients where veins might be less palpable.
- Patients with dark or thick skin that might obscure vein visibility.

Practical tips for using vein finders

- **Optimal room lighting:** Dimming ambient light can enhance the contrast and visibility of veins.
- **Skin preparation:** Clean the skin with an antiseptic wipe to remove any oils or lotions interfering with the device's function.
- **Device positioning:** Hold the device at the manufacturer's recommended distance for optimal visualization and use a steady hand.
- **Scan slowly:** Move the device slowly over the area of interest. This allows a comprehensive view of the venous structure.
- **Combine with palpation:** While the vein finder provides a visual guide, it is essential to palpate (feel) the vein to ensure it is suitable for venipuncture. This is particularly important for elderly patients or those with fragile veins.

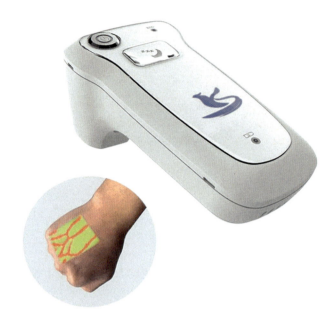

Fig-11-179. Another type of vein finder to visualize veins.

Benefits

- **Improved success rate:** Helps reduce the number of unsuccessful attempts, especially in patients with challenging veins, such as geriatric patients, pediatric patients, or patients with certain medical conditions.
- **Reduced pain and discomfort:** Fewer needle attempts mean less pain and discomfort for the patient.
- **Time-saving:** Locating veins quickly can save time, especially in emergencies.

Limitations and considerations

- **Depth of veins:** While very effective for superficial veins, deeper veins might still be challenging to visualize.
- **Device familiarity:** The practitioner must become familiar with the device to use it most effectively.
- **Cost:** High-end vein finders can be expensive, though more affordable options exist.

12

ADDITIONAL SUGGESTED READING

1. American Society of Anesthesiologists Task Force on Central Venous Access, Rupp SM, Apfelbaum JL, et al. Practice guidelines for central venous access: a report by the American Society of Anesthesiologists Task Force on Central Venous Access. Anesthesiology. 2012;116(3):539-573.
2. Anson JA. Vascular access in resuscitation: is there a role for the intraosseous route? Anesthesiology. 2014;120(4):1015-1031.
3. B Braun. Peripheral Cannulation and Venepuncture Training Programme Workbook.; 2017.
4. Beecham GB, Tackling G. Peripheral Line Placement. In: StatPearls. Treasure Island (FL): StatPearls Publishing; July 25, 2023.
5. Brideaux A, Murphy A, Chieng R. Ultrasound-guided peripheral intravenous cannulation. Radiopaedia.org.
6. Callejas A, Osiovich H, Ting JY. Use of peripherally inserted central catheters (PICC) via scalp veins in neonates. J Matern Fetal Neonatal Med. 2016;29(21):3434-3438.
7. Cheung E, Baerlocher MO, Asch M, Myers A. Venous access: a practical review for 2009. Can Fam Physician. 2009;55(5):494-496.
8. Chopra V. Central venous access: Device and site selection in adults. UpToDate. Published January 28, 2022. Accessed October 23, 2023. https://www.uptodate.com/contents/central-venous-access-device-and-site-selection-in-adults#H3537210845.
9. Cleveland Clinic. Blown Vein. Published January 12, 2023. Accessed October 20, 2023. https://my.clevelandclinic.org/health/diseases/24599-blown-vein.
10. Czarnik T, Gawda R, Perkowski T, Weron R. Supraclavicular approach is an easy and safe method of subclavian vein catheterization even in mechanically ventilated patients: analysis of 370 attempts. Anesthesiology. 2009;111(2):334-339.
11. Dev SP, Stefan RA, Saun T, Lee S. Videos in clinical medicine. Insertion of an intraosseous needle in adults. N Engl J Med. 2014;370(24):e35.
12. Dieter C. What Are The Different Types of IV Catheters? Penncare. Published August 25, 2022. Accessed October 20, 2023. https://www.penncare.net/2022/08/the-different-types-of-iv-catheters/.
13. Dietrich CF, Horn R, Morf S, et al. Ultrasound-guided central vascular interventions, comments on the European Federation of Societies for Ultrasound in Medicine and Biology guidelines on interventional ultrasound. J Thorac Dis. 2016;8(9):E851-E868.
14. Dong, MD M. A Manual for Ultrasound Guided Intravenous Access: Allay your Fears, Alleviate with Humor, Approach with Confidence. The Medicine Forum. 2023;24(1).
15. Dornhofer P, Kellar JZ. Intraosseous Vascular Access. Adult-Gerontology Acute Care Practice Guidelines, Second Edition. Published online June 5, 2023:579-580.
16. Dougherty L. Extravasation: prevention, recognition and management. Nurs Stand. 2010;24(52):48-60.
17. Eyssen A, Cops J, Hadzic A. Review of strategies to prevent infections related to ultrasound-guided nerve blocks and vascular access. Acta Anaesthesiologica Belgica. 2023 December; 74(4):281.
18. Farooq M. Ultrasound guidance for peripheral venous access. Anesthesiology. 2007;107(2):357.
19. Garcia-Expósito J, Masot O, Gros S, Botigué T, Roca J. Practical view of the topical treatment of peripheral venous catheter-related phlebitis: A scoping review. J Clin Nurs. 2022;31(7-8):783-797.
20. Giordano CR, Murtagh KR, Mills J, Deitte LA, Rice MJ, Tighe PJ. Locating the optimal internal jugular target site for central venous line placement. J Clin Anesth. 2016;33:198-202.
21. Kleidon TM, Schults J, Paterson R, Rickard CM, Ullman AJ. Comparison of ultrasound-guided peripheral intravenous catheter insertion with landmark technique in paediatric patients: A systematic review and meta-analysis. J Paediatr Child Health. 2022;58(6):953-961.
22. Konichezky S, Saguib S, Soroker D. Tracheal puncture. A complication of percutaneous internal jugular vein cannulation. Anaesthesia. 1983;38(6):572-574.
23. Lamperti M, Bodenham AR, Pittiruti M, et al. International evidence-based recommendations on ultrasound-guided vascular access. Intensive Care Med. 2012;38(7):1105-1117.
24. Lamperti M, Pittiruti M. II. Difficult peripheral veins: turn on the lights. Br J Anaesth. 2013;110(6):888-891.
25. Lavery I, Ingram P. Venepuncture: best practice. Nurs Stand. 2005;19(49).

26. Liu YT. How To Do Peripheral Vein Cannulation, Ultrasound-Guided. MSD Manual Professional Version. Published July 2023. Accessed October 23, 2023. https://www.msdmanuals.com/professional/critical-care-medicine/how-to-do-peripheral-vascularprocedures/how-to-do-peripheral-vein-cannulation,-ultrasound-guided.

27. Mbamalu D, Banerjee A. Methods of obtaining peripheral venous access in difficult situations. Postgrad Med J. 1999 Aug;75(886):459-62.

28. McGee DC, Gould MK. Preventing complications of central venous catheterization. N Engl J Med. 2003;348(12):1123-1133.

29. Moeckel D, Cresalia N, Vachharajani A. Umbilical Vein Catheterization. Neoreviews. 2023;14(8).

30. Ng M, Mark LKF, Fatimah L. Management of difficult intravenous access: a qualitative review. World J Emerg Med. 2022;13(6):467-478.

31. Periard D, Monney P, Waeber G, et al. Randomized controlled trial of peripherally inserted central catheters vs. peripheral catheters for middle duration in-hospital intravenous therapy. Journal of Thrombosis and Haemostasis. 2008;6(8):1281-1288.

32. Peripheral venous access. Amboss. Published April 6, 2023. Accessed October 23, 2023. https://www.amboss.com/us/knowledge/peripheral-venous-access.

33. Pitiriga V, Bakalis J, Theodoridou K, Kanellopoulos P, Saroglou G, Tsakris A. Lower risk of bloodstream infections for peripherally inserted central catheters compared to central venous catheters in critically ill patients. Antimicrob Resist Infect Control. 2022;11(1):137.

34. Practice Guidelines for Central Venous Access 2020: An Updated Report by the American Society of Anesthesiologists Task Force on Central Venous Access. Anesthesiology. 2020;132(1):8-43.

35. Privitera D, Mazzone A, Pierotti F, et al. Ultrasound-guided peripheral intravenous catheters insertion in patient with difficult vascular access: Short axis/out-of-plane versus long axis/in-plane, a randomized controlled trial. J Vasc Access. 2022;23(4):589-597.

36. Quadros AI, Stocco JGD, Cristoff C, Alcantara CB, Pimenta AM, Machado BGS. Adherence to central venous catheter maintenance bundle in an intensive care unit. Rev Esc Enferm USP. 2022;56:e20220077.

37. Reichman E.F. General Principles of Intravenous Access. In: Emergency Medicine Procedure. 2nd ed. McGraw Hill; 2013. Accessed October 20, 2023. https://accessemergencymedicine.mhmedical.com/content.aspx?bookid=683&sectionid=45343686.

38. Sandford H. Peripheral cannulation. Nurs Stand. 2008;22(52):59.

39. Saugel B, Scheeren TWL, Teboul JL. Ultrasound-guided central venous catheter placement: a structured review and recommendations for clinical practice. Crit Care. 2017;21(1):225.

40. Stone BA. Ultrasound guidance for peripheral venous access: a simplified seldinger technique. Anesthesiology. 2007;106(1):195.

41. Swaminathan L, Flanders S, Horowitz J, Zhang Q, O'Malley M, Chopra V. Safety and Outcomes of Midline Catheters vs Peripherally Inserted Central Catheters for Patients With Short-term Indications: A Multicenter Study. JAMA Intern Med. 2022;182(1):50-58.

42. Team Rapid Response. Rapid Guide to IV Starts for the RN and EMT. 3rd ed.; 2016.

43. The Royal Children's Hospital Melbourne. Intravenous access - Peripheral. Published September 2019. Accessed October 20, 2023. https://www.rch.org.au/clinicalguide/guideline_index/Intravenous_access_Peripheral/.

44. Tran T, Lund SB, Nichols MD, Kummer T. Effect of two tourniquet techniques on peripheral intravenous cannulation success: A randomized controlled trial. Am J Emerg Med. 2019;37(12):2209-2214.

45. Vera M. How to Start an IV? 50+ Tips & Techniques on IV Insertion. Nurseslabs. Published July 2, 2023. Accessed October 20, 2023. https://nurseslabs.com/how-to-start-an-iv-insertion-tips/.

46. Webster J, Osborne S, Rickard CM, Marsh N. Clinically-indicated replacement versus routine replacement of peripheral venous catheters. Cochrane Database Syst Rev. 2019;1(1):CD007798.

47. Witting MD, Schenkel SM, Lawner BJ, Euerle BD. Effects of vein width and depth on ultrasound-guided peripheral intravenous success rates. J Emerg Med. 2010;39(1):70-75.

48. Zitek T, Busby E, Hudson H, McCourt JD, Baydoun J, Slattery DE. Ultrasound-guided Placement of Single-lumen Peripheral Intravenous Catheters in the Internal Jugular Vein. West J Emerg Med. 2018;19(5):808-812.

Made in the USA
Las Vegas, NV
08 December 2024

13642515R00093